THE
FIELD&STREAM
Tackle Care and Repair Handbook

The *Field & Stream* Fishing and Hunting Library

FISHING

The Field & Stream *Baits and Rigs Handbook* by C. Boyd Pfeiffer
The Field & Stream *Bass Fishing Handbook* by Mark Sosin and Bill Dance
The Field & Stream *Fish Finding Guide* by Leonard M. Wright Jr.
The Field & Stream *Fishing Knots Handbook* by Peter Owen
The Field & Stream *Fly Fishing Handbook* by Leonard M. Wright Jr.
The Field & Stream *Tackle Care and Repair Handbook* by C. Boyd Pfeiffer

FORTHCOMING TITLES

HUNTING

The Field & Stream *Bow Hunting Handbook* by Bob Robb
The Field & Stream *Deer Hunting Handbook* by Jerome B. Robinson
The Field & Stream *Firearms Safety Handbook* by Doug Painter
The Field & Stream *Shooting Sports Handbook* by Thomas McIntyre
The Field & Stream *Turkey Hunting Handbook* by Philip Bourjaily
The Field & Stream *Upland Bird Hunting Handbook* by Bill Tarrant

THE
FIELD&STREAM
Tackle Care and Repair Handbook

C. Boyd Pfeiffer

THE LYONS PRESS

DEDICATION

To the memory of my dear wife,

JACKIE,

who always was and always will be
the inspiration for everything that I have done,
everything I do, and everything that I might accomplish.

10 9 8 7 6 5 4 3 2 1

Printed in the United States of America

Library of Congress Cataloging-in-Publication Data

Pfeiffer, C. Boyd.
    The field & stream tackle care and repair handbook / C. Boyd
Pfeiffer.
        p.   cm.—(Field & stream fishing and hunting library)
    Rev. ed. of Tackle care. 1987.
    Includes index.
    ISBN 1-55821-898-X
    1. Fishing tackle—Maintenance and repair.   I. Pfeiffer, C. Boyd.
Tackle care. II. Title.   III. Title: Field and stream tackle care
and repair handbook.   IV. Series.
SH447.R464   1999
799.1—dc21   98-49147
                                                  CIP

Contents

Acknowledgments

TACKLE CARE and maintenance is like fishing. You begin to learn about it at an early age, and continue to learn more throughout your whole life. I've had an interest in tackle care, maintenance, and repair since my first days of fishing, and thus learned from a lifetime of contact and experiences with friends, acquaintances, associates, camp fishing guides, store owners, and others. To them all, my thanks.

In the preparation this book, the tackle companies have all been helpful, filling out forms and answering questions about their end of the tackle maintenance business. In particular, Shakespeare, Daiwa, Penn, Mitchell, Zebco, Shimano, Browning, Plano, and Johnson have helped tremendously.

Zebco spokesmen were especially helpful in reviewing the reel maintenance section. Bill Norman Lures, Arbogast, Rebel, and Burke were most valuable with ideas on lure care and maintenance, as was Plano with input on tackleboxes. However, any errors or omissions remain my responsibility.

Special mention must be made of the staff of the Lyons Press, especially Nick Lyons.

Note to the Reader

This book is as complete as I can make it, short of including encyclopedic details on the repair instructions for every type of reel ever made! I am, however, interested in hearing about more, new, and different methods of tackle care, maintenance, and repair, along with those of tackle making and modification. Readers interested in sharing or exchanging ideas may contact me through the publisher.

Caution

I have made every effort to include and describe tackle care, maintenance, and repair procedures that are not only easy but safe. Any tackle care, maintenance, or repair procedure, however, does involve the handling of tackle and tackle parts, and the use of tools.

Naturally, in undertaking any of these tasks, some familiarity with tackle and tools is paramount for safety.

The Care of
Fishing Tackle

TACKLE CARE begins when tackle is bought. If you buy a spool of line and place it on the rear shelf of your car where it will be in the sun for a long time, you are setting the stage for that line to fail when you take it out of the clear container to use it. When you buy a reel, mount it on a rod then, and throw it into a car trunk where it will rattle around with jacks and tire chains, don't be surprised if that rod or reel is damaged when you take it out to fish.

Each type of tackle—rods, reels, lines, and various types of lures and accessories—must be cared for differently if it is to retain its usefulness. Some of the basics for this follow.

RODS

Rods are particularly susceptible to breakage, primarily in car and home doors. At home, rods should be stored in special racks or rod cases (more on home storage tips later) and kept away from heat, humidity, and out of home traffic patterns where they might be damaged. When taken out for fishing, two- or multipiece rods should be broken down to prevent breakage. One-piece rods or rods that you do not want to break down should only be taken outside after a screen or storm door is locked open or when someone holds the door for you. Many rod tips are broken when they get caught by an inadvertently slammed door.

Rod Cases and Bags

The best place to keep any rod is in a bag or tube, which either comes with the rod or is available separately. The most protection is provided by using a fitted bag and a plastic or aluminum case or tube. The soft bag protects the rod guides and blank from scratches and nicks. The hard case protects the rod from major blows. Bags should have compartments for each section of the rod so that the sections will not scratch each other. Some rods, primarily expensive fly rods, will come with a bag and aluminum case. Other rods only come with a cloth or vinyl bag or plastic case. These are less effective than a bag and case, but better than no case at all.

Rod in bag in small PVC tube.

Rods without cases or bags can still be protected. It is easy to make a bag from mill-run ends and flannel remnants, which are soft, inexpensive, and readily available from fabric shops. Flannel is easy to sew on a sewing machine, but be sure to allow for the largest guide or the trigger of a casting-rod handle so the rod will easily fit the case. It is not necessary to add special ties. Just make the bag several inches longer than the longest rod section so that the end can be folded over and held in place with a rubber band.

Travel cases that hold several or more rods are also available. Rods should be separated by either placing them in cloth bags or rolling them up in a flannel sheeting so that the sections are not touching. Most travel cases range from 3 to $4\frac{1}{2}$ inches in diameter and in lengths (some telescoping) up to 8 feet. Rod cases such as these are available from companies such as Rod Caddy (Bead Chain), Plano, Fenwick, Flambeau, Wright & McGill, and other manufacturers.

Home Storage of Rods

Rod storage at home is important, because that is where many breaks and tackle accidents occur. Some storage possibilities are:

Vertical Storage This type of storage is great because it keeps the rods up, usually along a wall or in a special rod rack, and prevents a set or bend from developing that could damage the rod. There are two ways to keep them vertical. One is to hang the rod by its tiptop or upper guide; the second is by fitting it into a commercial rod holder or rack. The problem with hanging any except light rods is that in time, the rod's weight can be too heavy for the tiptop joint. This joint has the tube of the rod tip glued to the rod blank. In time, the weight of the rod could pull the rod free of the tip.

Hanging the rod by the first guide on an L hanger (available by that name from any hardware store, and in several sizes) solves this problem. A heavy rod with a light tip, such as a West Coast live-lining or albacore rod, could still exert a

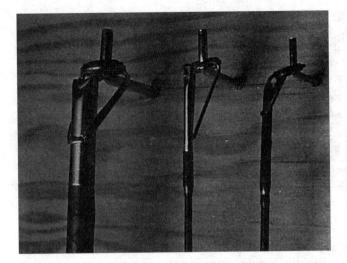

Some anglers use right-angle cup hooks to hold and hang rods by the tips. If doing this, do *not* keep reels on the rods, since the weight will make for too much strain on the rod's tip joint.

bend on the rod, since the hanging point is not in line with the rod blank, but at an angle from the blank at the rim of the guide ring. Too heavy a rod might also, in time, weaken the guide or guide wrap.

An additional problem with any storage system like this is that for the angler with many rods, they do take up space—usually wall space. The obvious advantage is that the rod is ready to grab on a moment's notice. One solution to the space problem is to make racks—like the fold-up racks used to sell posters—mounted with L brackets to hold the rods.

This method can also be used another way, in which the rod rests on a base support or socket and is held in place at the upper end of the rod. Foam, spring-lock mechanisms, brush-type holders, and rubber grippers are available in standard rod racks from fishing-tackle manufacturers. You can build vertical racks of any length for any number of rods by making sockets for the butt cap of the rod and using a clasp to hold the upper part of the rod blank. Butt-cap sockets can be made with a hole saw or Forstner bit (a special woodworker's blind-bottoming drill bit) in a 2 × 4, using 2-inch PVC pipe-end caps, or plastic caps from household spray cans. Upper rod clamps can be made of foam, spring locks, broom spring holders (cover the metal fingers with tape or tubing, though), and similar holding devices available at hardware stores.

Horizontal Storage Horizontal storage is fine, provided that the rods are supported properly, either on a flat surface or at several support points. Rods can also be stored flat in their cases, but take the end cap off to prevent moisture from accumulating, which can bubble the finish on the rod. (This also occurs when a wet rod is cased.)

Other systems that work well are a high rafter shelf in a basement, on which rods can be placed flat, or a system of hooks, or hooks and loops, to hang rods at the handle and at a balance point farther up the rod.

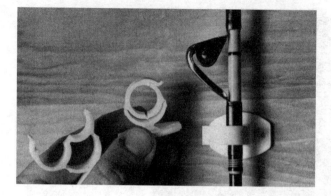

Snap-open holders like these are ideal to hold the upper end of rods. They hold a rod securely yet won't mar it.

    A perforated board with hooks can provide similar horizontal support along a wall. In any of these arrangements, be sure the rod is supported to prevent severe bends. This often means that the spacing between the two support points will vary according to the type of rod. A long surf rod, for example, might have a 6- to 8-foot separation. An ultralight panfish rod might need less than 3 feet of space between supports. Flat storage in a garage or carport is also good, particularly for long rods (such as those used for surf or jetty fishing), if they are protected from theft and rodents.

Author with his overhead basement storage of rods. The hook-and-loop system works well to hold a number of rods horizontally.

Some fishing-tackle companies make horizontal rod racks. These consist of two foam racks into which the rod sections are secured.

I use the loop-and-hook arrangement, storing rods on the rafters in my basement. The loops are heavy nylon cord, stapled into a board. Each loop is 3 inches deep. I use 6 inches of cord, with a 2-inch space between loops. The other end of the rod is held by 1¼-inch cup hooks, also spaced 2 inches apart. For easiest construction, make up the brackets on separate lathing strips in the length you need and tack the bracket into the rafters.

Car Storage of Rods

The best place for a rod in any vehicle is in a case. I've seen enough uncased rods break in closing car windows and cluttered trunks to last me a lifetime.

Lacking cases, rods are best stored out of the way—broken down into two or more sections across the back window shelf, along one side of the car (be careful of windows and doors, though), or stretched through the center of the car in hatchback models. On wagons or vans, a horizontal racking system along the roof line is great, because it provides enough space for any but the longest rods, holds them generally out of sight, and keeps them where they cannot be damaged. Berkley and Rod Saver have such systems. These have a snap-down end to hold the handle and a ring or strap-down end to hold the rod's other end. The ring idea is the best choice, although you must take care when removing a rod so the guides won't catch on the ring. A similar homemade arrangement uses rope or aluminum straps at the handle and PVC pipe or golf tubes to hold the tip end. Up to 10 rods can be held in most vehicles this way.

Boat Storage of Rods

Rod breakage in boats usually results from too few rod holders or racks to secure the rods when they aren't being used. Rods in boats must be kept so that they are out of the way, yet instantly available. The best storage spots on small boats are

Large rods are best protected for car travel by storing them on outside rod racks (as shown) rather than trying to cram them into small cars.

Rods and reels are best protected on boats by using some sort of rod holder, as shown on this small center-console fishing boat. These rod holders are under the wide gunwale to protect the tackle. This allows you to carry ready-rigged rods and reels and still protect them.

along the gunwales. On bass boats there is often little space here; Velcro straps, attached to the front deck to hold rods down, are the best solution. On larger boats (usually 16 feet and longer) the best spots for rods are underneath the wide gunwales that these boats often have. These areas can hold horizontally racked rods in ring-and-clip, clip and PVC pipe, or similar systems. The best storage solution is to place the rod tip into a sleeve or tube and hold the handle or butt with a spring clip or elastic cord. That way, the rod is completely protected but is readily available. The arrangement is similar to pulling a sword from a sheath.

Another solution, used primarily on center-console boats for obvious reasons, is vertical rod racks. These use butt sockets and foam or spring clips to hold the rod blank upright. Vertical racks are best for rigged rods, but use them only if there is enough space around the rod rack for easy passage. For under-gunwale rod mounts, a wide gunwale is necessary to prevent a hook from snagging pant legs.

Travel with Rods

Travel with rods requires large-diameter rod cases. Use a cloth bag for each rod, then put them in the case. I use a large sheet of flannel and roll up the rods in it. The flannel must be several feet longer on each end than the longest rod. Lay the flannel out on the floor, lay the rods out in the middle of the cloth, fold the ends over the rods, and roll up, making sure that a layer of flannel protects each rod section. Use straps or ties to hold the bundle together and place it in the large travel case. Label the case, both inside and out, with your name and address.

REELS

Reels are compact and sturdy for their intended purpose, but they must also have adequate care if they are to last a long time. And they can last a long time.

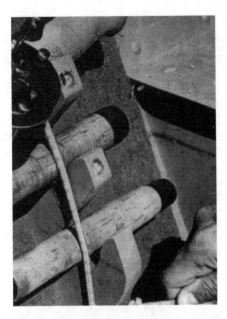

The rack end of rod holders usually consists of homemade wood racks to hold and support the rod handle. The bungee (elastic) cord shown holds the rods down while running the boat.

When traveling, rods must be protected by using a large-diameter travel rod tube. For best results, wrap up the rods in a large flannel cloth before storing in the rod tube.

A friend recently brought me a bait-casting reel that he had been actively using for more than 20 years. The reel needed a new pinion gear, and we added a new main gear and spool for insurance. It should now last another 20 years. But this friend takes care of his tackle, regularly checking, cleaning, and lubricating it.

When stored or not used, all reels should have the drags backed off until the drag is loose. Drags are made up of alternating soft (usually fiber or leather) and hard (metal) washers, with the metal washers keyed alternately to the spool and the reel shaft. The pressure on the drag screw creates resistance in the layers of washers to turning, thus creating the drag on the spool. Leaving a drag tight deforms the soft washers and can make a drag less effective, erratic, and jumpy.

Poor drag performance is the main reason for lost fish and broken lines when playing a fish. Similarly, casting reels should also have the cast control slightly loosened to reduce pressure on the bearings and spool axle.

Reel Bags and Cases

Most reels break when they are dropped or when something bangs into them. The simple solution here is to keep a reel as protected as possible. Reels should be washed after use (more about this in chapter 3, Reel Maintenance), dried, and stored in a tackle- or reel box or protective bag. Leather bags are not good, particularly for saltwater reels, because they hold moisture and salt that can corrode the reel. The best bags are made of cloth or nylon and have a drawstring top.

An alternative to a bag is to store the reels in a clean, dry tacklebox when not in use. Some tackle companies make hard- or soft-sided containers specifically for carrying reels.

On many spinning reels, the bail and/or handle folds down to make the reel more compact for easy storage. This should be done whenever and wherever a reel is to be stored, since these parts are also the most susceptible to damage.

Reel Storage: Home, Cars, and Boats

Keep reels at home in boxes, bags, tackle bags, on shelves (protected from dust), or hanging from perforated board hooks for ready availability and display. Back off the drag as outlined above. (Cleaning, maintenance, and line spooling are covered in chapter 5, Accessory Maintenance.)

The best storage in cars is in a *dry* tacklebox or similar hard container, preferably with the reel in a bag. Bag protection is particularly important if there are several reels kept in the same compartment, or if the reel is stored with other accessories that might scratch or damage it.

In boats, keep reels in tackleboxes or boat storage compartments. Better still, mount reels on a rod and store them in rod racks.

Travel with Reels

Reels can be easily packed for travel. They are best stored with the bails, handles, and any other parts folded down, protected in reel bags, and stored in a hard case or tacklebox. For air travel, pack reels in a regular hard-sided suitcase or in the center of a duffel bag where they are protected by layers of clothing.

LINES

Line *must* be replaced regularly. Some tournament fishermen replace line after each hard fight or trophy fish. Bass pros often change it after each day of tournament fishing or after each tournament. Most of us need not go to that extreme, but line should be changed each year. If you don't, the line will eventually twist, become brittle, or break from abrasion—all of which can result in lost fish. And lost fish are not the only casualty from inadequate line care. In a poll of a number of manufacturers, most reported that many reel problems are caused by poor, old, or insufficient line on the reel. Insufficient line makes casting difficult and distance impossible. Twisted line can get caught around the rotor shaft of spinning and spincast reels, or under the spool of some casting and offshore models. That not only ruins the line, but can ruin reel parts. The original problem, of course, is not the reel, but the line.

Line care is simple. For monofilament lines, simply keep them out of the sun, away from moisture, and in a cool, dry, dark place. If you buy reel-fill spools and use them immediately, all these precautions are unnecessary. Storage of bulk line spools, however, is important.

Experts, such as those from Stren and Berkley, major fishing-line manufacturers, agree that most things that come in contact with monofilament will not harm it. Greases, oils, other lubricants, suntan and aftershave lotions, perfume, deodorants, demoisturizing sprays (WD-40, CRC), gasoline, and so on, will not damage monofilament. Battery acid, though, will ruin all line.

Fly lines are different because most of them consist of a PVC coating over a braided core. This coating can be damaged by many of the above, especially suntan lotions and gasoline, and also insect repellent. In short, any strong organic solvent or chlorinated hydrocarbon can harm the PVC coating. All such substances should naturally be kept away from line where and when possible—even mono—because they could be absorbed by the line and impart a smell that might repel fish. There are some exceptions, although any contact with line by such products is best avoided.

LURES

That lures last as long as they do and look as good as they do after being repeatedly thrown into water, and bounced off rocks, logs, and barnacles, is nothing short of a miracle.

Store lures in tackleboxes. Ideally, each lure should be in a separate compartment to prevent scratches from the hooks of other lures. But for most of us, this is impossible. Most anglers organize their tackleboxes with adjustable compartment dividers so that several or more lures fit into each slot. Sort lures by type, though, if for no other reason than to keep hard-plastic and wood crankbaits (plugs), soft-plastic lures, worms, and spinnerbaits with their skirts separated.

The reasoning for this is simple. Soft-plastic lures release a solvent (the plasticizer used to make them soft) that will attack hard plastics such as those used in crankbaits. Soft plastics will even attack the paint on wood plugs. They will also damage any tackleboxes that are not labeled "wormproof," although most boxes today are not affected by worms.

In addition, soft plastics should be kept isolated by color and type because

Boots—short hip boots and waders—can be either stored in a plastic bag and in a box or hung up as shown. Proper hanging will reduce the wrinkles, which are a main cause of rubber breakdown and ozone damage.

direct contact of differently colored soft plastics will result in the colors "bleeding" from one lure to another.

The rubber, plastic, and vinyl skirts used in spinnerbaits can become gummy and harm hard lures. Soft plastics also attack spinnerbait skirts and the paint on the leadhead. Jigs with similar skirts will also react and be affected the same way.

ACCESSORIES

Accessories such as nets, gaffs, creels, boots, tackleboxes, and other fishing equipment also need care. This usually involves commonsense storage and handling. Hang up nets in a clean, dry area. Left in the bottom of a boat or on a damp garage floor, the bag might need replacement before fishing next spring.

Protect rubber and hip boots and waders from ozone. Many boot manufacturers recommend storing them in a sealed plastic bag that has had as much of the air as possible removed. Many anglers hang their boots up; the main caution here is guarding against folds or wrinkles that might stress the rubber and provide a place for ozone to attack the material.

Keep gaffs clean and stored where they are out of the way and can't get damaged or hurt anyone.

More and more fishing accessories run on batteries. These include portable depthsounders, line strippers, flashlights, pH meters, thermometers, GPS, and so on. Batteries can leak when not used, so remove them from such equipment when they won't be used for a long period.

Rod Maintenance

GOOD ROD MAINTENANCE can be as simple as visually checking the rod, or as complicated as occasionally recoating the rod wraps on the guides or even refinishing the whole rod. More extensive work involves replacing guides, handles, and tiptops, fixing loose reel seats, and the like (all this is covered in chapter 6, Rod Repair).

Admittedly, just where maintenance leaves off and repair work begins is subject to interpretation. A new coating on a guide wrap might be maintenance for some and repair for others. I've taken the position that anything that maintains a rod in its original working condition is maintenance. Anything that requires actual removal, replacement, or fixing of the rod or rod parts is repair and will be covered under that chapter.

Rods have no working or moving parts other than the hood on the reel seat and the rollers on roller guides on offshore rods. They are simple to check and maintain. Problems with rods and reels arrive when the reels are left on rods, particularly after saltwater fishing. This allows salt to build up in the crevices around the reel seat/reel foot, and will usually corrode these parts. If the reel seat is not cleaned regularly, it can weaken the seat and movable hood, corrode the threads in the barrel and hood, and lock up the seat and make reel removal impossible. The argument could be made that this won't happen on rod/reel combinations in which the reel is all graphite and the seat is graphite or stainless steel. Reel seats of graphite fill and stainless steel are on many modern factory rods and even on custom rods in which the Fuji FPS style of reel seat or a similar design is used.

In other seats, corrosion can begin where metal reel seats come in contact with metal reel feet. The dissimilar metals set up a galvanic action, which produces an electrical current that will corrode both metals. The best answer is to remove the reel from the rod so that both can be washed independently.

Ideally, rods should be washed off after each fishing trip. This, however, depends upon fishing conditions. When fishing in clear, clean fresh water such regular care is unnecessary. If the fresh water is murky or filled with algae or weeds, such cleaning is a must. Algae or silt from the murky water will be picked up on the fishing line and deposited on the guides, around the guide feet, and on the rod blank. When fishing in salt water, salt spray will coat the rod, so washing with fresh water is a must to keep the rod functional.

How you wash the rod depends upon how dirty and salt caked it is. For light cleaning, a simple spray with a garden hose is ideal. Even in saltwater areas, most cleaning tables or boat docks have a freshwater hose for this purpose. For very dirty rods, scrub with a light brush or rag and give particular attention to the areas around the guides, guide rings, guide feet, and reel seat. To keep the reel seat working, it is best to screw the movable hood all the way to one end of the barrel, scrub the threads on the barrel with a rag or washcloth, screw the movable hood to the other end, and repeat the cleaning. It takes only a few minutes and will clean away any salt or scum. Roller guides such as those by AFTCO also require special cleaning around the rollers to keep them free of salt and to keep them rolling. This is easy to do with an old toothbrush, working with soapy water around these fittings.

One method that I use is to take all my rods into the shower with me at the end of each day. It is easy to clean me and the fishing rods at the same time. Use a washcloth around the reel seat and guides; use the old toothbrush on the rollers and reel seats. After washing, I rinse the rods completely, stand them in the shower stall until dry, then store them in the basement.

Checking Rods

How often you check a rod, and how thoroughly you check it, depends upon many things, including how rough you are on tackle, how rough a particular fishing trip was, and whether you were fishing in salt water or around murky or alga-filled water. A check after each trip might be good. In other situations, an annual check is enough.

A careful check of any rod is suggested under the following conditions:

1. After any trip in which the rod has been abused, knocked around, possibly damaged.

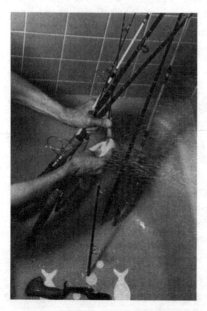

Rinse all rods after each trip, especially if used in salt water. These rods are being rinsed in the shower, using a wash rag to give particular attention to the guides and reel seats.

2. When fishing extensively with light tackle for big fish, because such conditions can severely strain tackle.

3. Anytime you have a problem casting, fighting fish, pumping a fish, holding the reel on the reel seat, and so on. Such conditions indicate a problem with the rod or reel.

4. Anytime you see something wrong with the rod, such as a loose thread on a guide wrap, wobbly guide, gouged cork handle, and so on.

5. When you have been fishing in scummy, alga- or weed-filled water, such conditions will coat the rod with scum that can cause line wear in time.

6. After fishing extensively in salt water, especially if using roller guides, because rollers can become nonfunctional and clogged with salt spray.

7. Anytime you fall down with, or on, a rod, because the blank can fracture or guides can bend or break.

Things to check on a rod, and possible corrections, include:

Butt Cap Check for damage or looseness. If it is a metal cap, check for any signs of corrosion or pitting, especially if fishing in salt water. Butt caps often come loose. An easy solution is to remove the butt cap, use a knife or file to scrape out any loose glue, and reglue it. It is best to abrade the cap's inside to provide more tooth for the glue, and to use a good glue such as a 24-hour epoxy. Epoxy rod finish is also excellent to use for rubber or soft-plastic butt caps, because it is more flexible and will give with the rod butt.

Handles and Grips Handles and grips can become dirty and require nothing more than a cleaning, or can become damaged, requiring repair. Cleaning a handle or grip requires more than the simple scrubdown for rods described in chapter 1, although a regular washing will do a lot to keep grips clean and usable.

Cork grips and handles in time become discolored from repeated handling. To restore a cork grip to the original, light-buff appearance, sand with a fine sandpaper. Use only fine or extra-fine grades because coarser paper will roughen the finish and remove cork. Take care to avoid scratching any other parts of the rod such as butt caps, reel seats, and rod blanks. The simple solution here is to wrap these parts with masking tape and remove it when you are finished sanding.

Some synthetic grips (Hypalon, Foamlite, and similar names are used for this pliable spongy material) become shiny and slick in time and lose their holding surface. To restore the grips to their original finish, sand them with a medium or coarse sandpaper. Again, protect other parts of the rod with several layers of masking tape.

Wood handles on some boat and jetty rods generally require little more than a good scrubbing to keep them in good order. Most of these handles have a protective finish of varnish or epoxy, and this might become worn or flaky. Scrubbing with a hard nylon brush or nylon scrubbing pad will loosen and remove any flaking, but a true restoration is really in the repair department and involves removing the old finish and refinishing.

Aluminum handles such as those on offshore and boat rods can only be scrubbed clean, because abrasive materials will scratch and may remove the anodizing that protects the aluminum finish.

Factory handles, such as those molded for casting rods, can only be cleaned. For these use a scrub rag, nylon scrub pad, or other nonabrasive cleaner.

When you are cleaning and checking handles and grips, also look thoroughly for damage that might require repairs. Cork grips are subject to gouging, crushing, cracking, and splitting. Most of this is a result of blows to the handle that damage the cork. You can repair gouges, replace cork rings, fill holes, and so on (see chapter 6, Rod Repair).

Hypalon can't really be repaired, but seldom suffers damage the way cork does. Check for cuts, cracks, and dents, which can occur when trolling rods are placed in boat rod holders where rod pressure dents the grip. Wood handles can also become splintered or dented, but they are generally easy to repair with standard woodworking practices.

Reel Seats It is particularly important to clean reel seats thoroughly after each use, especially after fishing in salt or muddy water. Reel seats are made of aluminum, chrome-plated brass, and graphite or graphite-filled plastics. If they are cleaned regularly, a check can consist of nothing more than a simple examination of the reel seat for corrosion, scratches, loosening, split hoods, worn barrel threads, and the like. Most of these problems are prevented by careful cleaning. Corrosion usually starts with a scratch or break in the finish that allows water to penetrate and the metal to oxidize. If this occurs, the only maintenance is constant cleaning and checking.

When working with a bare metal, such as chrome over brass, metal polishes are best for removing corrosion and keeping the reel seat attractive. If working with an anodized reel seat, carefully rub away any corrosion and clean regularly to prevent heavy oxidation from returning. Using metal polishes cavalierly will wear the anodizing, and the seat will lose the color and protection provided by the coating.

To avoid scratches, keep the rod protected in bags and/or cases and in holders at home or in boats. Avoid allowing the rod to come in contact with the ground, sand, and equipment or tools that might scratch the seat. Loose reel seats are a result of poor gluing and are a repair problem.

Split hoods can result from flimsy manufacture, but they are often caused by too much pressure on the hood. The split is almost always on slip-over reel seats with swaged hoods. (Swaged hoods are those made by taking a round collar and using dies to force it into a shape in which a recess is formed to hold the end of the reel foot.) The split often occurs along an area of maximum stress, such as the edge of the recess for the reel foot. This is impossible to repair; the only solution is to replace the hood or, more likely, the entire reel seat.

Rod Blank The rod blank is the "pole" that makes up the basis of the rod. Maintenance involves nothing more than keeping the rod clean, keeping it protected, and avoiding blows that will damage the hollow blank construction of any glass, graphite, boron, or composite rod. (A few rods are solid or have solid tips or sections. Any solid rod or part is less subject to damage, but a hard or crushing blow will still ruin it.)

Use a soft cloth to wash the rod regularly so the factory finish will be preserved. In time, some finishes have been known to flake and look like a bad case of peeling sunburn. There is no maintenance program to prevent this, and the poor appearance will not affect performance or action. The only solution is to remove the old finish with fine steel wool and refinish the rod with a brush-on or spray epoxy. Be warned, however, that no home refinish can equal the oven-baked factory coating.

Guides Guides are difficult to clean properly, what with the frames, added supports, small-sized rings, and light-wire construction, but some tips will make it easier. First, guides should be cleaned often with a rag or washcloth as outlined in chapter 1 on general care. Periodically, depending upon usage and need, it helps to clean the guides with an old toothbrush or similar small brush. Use these to work around and clean the junction of the frame with the wrapped guide foot, the frame's junction with the wire ring, and the guide ring itself. Use the same methods to clean roller guides, then wash, rinse, and liberally oil the roller and the bushings and pins that hold it. It is easy to remove the small screws holding the roller and bushing in place for a more through cleaning.

Small bends in the guide frame are usually easy to see, and can be straightened with small wide-jaw pliers. Guide rings are more difficult to check. Guides that have an inner wire ring (stainless steel/hard chrome is most commonly used) will develop grooves in time from fishing line passing over the same spot on the guide. Initial grooving is difficult to detect, although the deeper grooves that come with time are readily apparent. Guides with inner rings of ceramic, aluminum oxide, silicon carbide, Hardloy, and similar materials will not groove, but a blow to the guide can crack them. The nylon shock ring holding the inner ring in place keeps the crack from showing or the guide ring from falling out, but the crack can rapidly damage line.

The best way to check for cracks is to pull a fine material through the guide and see if it catches. Nylon stockings, cotton balls, or tissue paper will all work. Grooved guides in chrome rings must be replaced, because the line running in the groove will constantly be abraded. Cracked aluminum, silicon carbide, or Hardloy rings should be replaced, but if the single crack is in a position that will not catch the line on retrieve (close to the rod in a spinning rod and far from the rod in a casting rod), you can probably live with it for some time without damaging the line.

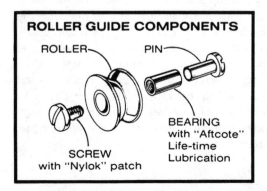

ROLLER GUIDE COMPONENTS

ROLLER

PIN

SCREW
with "Nylok" patch

BEARING
with "Aftcote"
Life-time
Lubrication

Parts of roller guides can be taken apart and cleaned, then reassembled. *Courtesy of AFTCO.*

Tiptops Tiptops are special guides that fit on the end of a rod. The checks and minor adjustments possible with guides also apply here. The wire support frames can be bent into shape if deformed, and the rings should be checked for grooves or cracks.

Ferrules The self-ferrules of glass-to-glass or graphite-to-graphite used in most modern rods require little care or maintenance. To keep them working properly, periodically coat the male portion of the ferrule with candle wax. The wax—usually a mixture of paraffin and beeswax—seats the ferrules without slippage and also keeps them from binding together. When waxing ferrules make sure that they are first free of grime or dirt.

Metal ferrules or rod joints are seldom seen today because of the influx of self-ferrules, glass-to-glass or graphite-to-graphite. Older metal ferrules sometimes become stuck because dirt and grime can make them difficult to seat properly or remove once seated. To correct this, wash them carefully with a soapy solution to cut any grease or grime. If they are still sticking, and not deformed in any way, consider lightly polishing them with very fine steel wool. Buff sparingly, and clean and check the ferrule after every few strokes. The only thing worse than a too-tight ferrule is one too loose.

Ferrules can lose their shape. The best solution is to replace them (see chapter 6, Rod Repair), but a simple Band-Aid-type repair can be done by inserting a ferrule into a large drill chuck and, using the key for the chuck, re-forming the ferrule back into an almost-round shape. Because there are three jaws in drill chucks and they are often slightly concave, this method works well as a temporary solution to a bent ferrule.

Another maintenance problem that can develop with self-spigot-type ferrules is when the edge of the female ferrule seats against the lower lip of the male portion because of excessive wear. When this happens, the ferrule will begin to loosen because the friction that holds the two in place is lost. To fix this, use a file or emery board to file down the end of the male ferrule. Be careful, because you only need about a $\frac{1}{8}$- to $\frac{3}{16}$-inch clearance, and excessive filing will cut into the thread wrap necessary to maintain hoop strength.

Rod Wraps There are two types of rod wraps: functional and decorative. Functional wraps are threads that hold the guide feet on the rod or wrap ferrules. Decorative wraps adorn the rod handle, at the tiptop, and at any other spot on the rod.

Guides are not glued to the rod, so the thread wraps are the only thing holding them in place and in line with the reel and each other. Ferrule wraps are necessary to give the rod blank hoop strength. Hoop strength helps maintain the hollow rod blank in a round configuration and prevents the blank from collapsing when the rod is bent, such as when casting or fighting a fish. This strength is built into a rod with transverse fibers in the rod blank that help hold the round shape. The ends, however, where rods join at built-in ferrules are particularly vulnerable to breakage (especially when they are glass-to-glass or graphite-to-graphite). The wrap here prevents the ends from splintering and other damage.

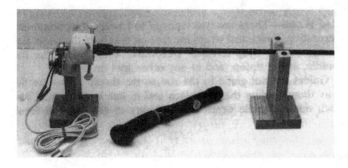

A professional-type rod-wrapping device will hold any type of rod for slow turning and curing of epoxy.

Replacing these wraps is a repair job (see chapter 6, Rod Repair). Often, however, this repair can be avoided by carefully checking and maintaining the protective coating on the wraps. At one time these coatings were varnish but today they are usually thicker, harder, and more durable epoxies. Wear often comes when a rod rests with too much pressure in a rod holder, against boat seats or gunwales, and so on at the point where these wraps are located. After the finish is worn through, the wraps begin to fray. To avoid this, refinish any or all wraps with an epoxy when they become slightly worn or show signs of wear. Areas around the wrap's edge are particularly vulnerable because fraying begins at this point.

Refinish only the thread wrap, because the rest of the rod, whether custom-made from a rod blank or a factory model, has a baked-on finish that is far better than anything that can be done at home.

A new finish can go over any old finish. Old finishes can be varnish, spar varnish, epoxy, manufacturer UV-activated finishes, one-part air-dry urethanes, two-part air-dry urethanes, and similar coatings. Varnish, epoxy, and some urethane finishes available to the hobbyist will all work. Varnish is seldom used anymore, except by fishermen who like to build and maintain rods that boast traditional construction and appointments. Many rod manufacturers use UV-activated urethanes. Some experts feel that these look great initially, but break down and get cloudy in time and require replacement or refinishing. These coatings are not available to fisher-

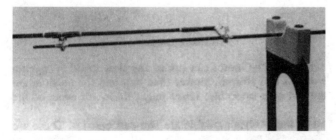

In some cases it is necessary to refinish an entire rod using spray epoxy. In this case, the rod cannot rest on the rod support as in refinishing individual wraps. To solve this, run a short rod blank or dowel through the guides, tape them, and let the dowel or rod run on the support as shown. This way, the entire rod can be sprayed.

men, because they are highly toxic and their application requires special machinery to emit UV rays for curing.

No special tools or machinery are needed to refinish rod wraps, but if you have a rod-wrapping motor (low-rpm motor) or a rotisserie motor for your barbecue grill, it will help. The first slowly turns rods while the wrap finish cures, the second can be jury-rigged with a butt cap to hold the rod in the blind square hole in the rotisserie motor. In most cases, the rod must be supported above the midpoint with an additional bracket. You can support the rod on a small cardboard box with a V cut into it (on the same plane or level as the rod motor), or cut a strip from a plastic milk carton as a bed on which the rod can ride to prevent scratches. The motor can run at any slow speed between a range of 1 and 60 rpm. Slower than that and the finish might sag and not cure smoothly; faster might throw off some of the finish.

Most of the finishes available are two-part epoxies. These are also the best coatings available to the home hobbyist because they can be used with one coat. To assure a good new finish on top of the old, clean the wrap finish carefully with soap and water to remove dirt. Allow it to dry overnight, because a thorough cleaning often leaves water around the junction of the guide frame with the guide foot wrap. For proper adhesion, buff the remaining rod finish with fine steel wool. To prevent scratching the rod blank, cover it immediately adjacent to the wrap with a layer or two of masking tape. (Any misses with the steel wool will hit the tape, not the rod finish.) Once buffed, remove the tape, clean the area thoroughly, and apply the epoxy finish.

Epoxy finishes are two part and they set up rapidly so they must be mixed and used carefully, according to Roger Seiders, president of Flex Coat, a Texas manufacturer of rod finishes and accessories for rod building, maintenance, and repair.

Seiders feels that epoxies mix best when they are at 80° to 90° F. He uses the heat from a lightbulb to gently warm the separate bottles before mixing.

"If you heat it," noted Seiders, "it will mix better, draw up into the thread better, form less bubbles, and be stronger."

Some mixes, such as Seiders's Flex Coat, come with syringes, although separate syringes or small mixing cups are available for mixing other epoxies. The small pharmaceutical or 1-ounce disposable medicine cups are ideal for this,

An alternative is to use ball-bearing swivels and attach the rod tip to a support via several swivels. This also allows spraying the entire rod, since the swivels will allow the rod to turn.

because the two parts can be easily measured. Do *not* use medical syringes, because these are usually lubricated with a silicon coating. Silicon causes extensive problems when using epoxies.

When mixing the two parts, stir them thoroughly. Seiders used to recommend two minutes of stirring, but has revised that to a visual check of the solution as you mix it. He explained that during the mixing process, Flex Coat will first become cloudy and then clear as it becomes mixed. With good light this is visible. Other finishes may not have this characteristic, in which case a thorough, timed mix is best. It also is best to use a round mixing stick because flat sticks pick up tiny air bubbles and incorporate them into the mix. If possible, fold the two parts of epoxy together to minimize bubbles. Don't beat it to a froth; that will create and increase bubbles.

Once mixed, any two-part epoxy will heat up, hastening the catalytic reaction that will cause the mixture to cure. To slow this and prolong "pot life" so that you can get the mix carefully on the rod wrap, pour the mixture onto something flat. This will get it "out of mass," help eliminate any residual bubbles, and control the curing time. Seiders suggested using aluminum foil because it is cheap, disposable, and helps dissipate the mix's heat buildup, further prolonging the working life.

Another way to dissipate the bubbles is to blow or breathe on the surface. Experts are unsure why this works, but it does. Their theories include a change in vapor pressure, the carbon dioxide in our breath, and the unsettling of the surface tension.

When the mix is ready, spread the finish with a fine brush. Disposable brushes are best, because they are cheap and perform well. Working in good light, cover the end of the wrap, making sure that the epoxy touches the rod all the way around the blank so water cannot reach the threads. Similarly, work the finish under the guide frame and around the junction of the guide frame with the wrap. Make sure that the entire wrap is finished. When you use a good strong light, you will be able to see the sheen of the finish as you turn the rod and apply the finish to any missed spots. If working on a long rod, or on one with many guides, begin at the butt end, because it will be easier to apply any curing and thickening finish to the smaller wraps on the rod's tip end.

Once all the finish is applied, place the rod in the motorized turner and allow it to turn for several hours. Make one last check to make sure that no spots are missed and fill in any gaps. If you don't have a motor, you can still finish a rod. Apply a thin coat of finish and turn the rod 90° every 5 to 10 minutes. (Television specials are great for this, because they have enough interruptions to permit you to make each turn and last long enough for most rods to set up.) Curing will take about 24 hours, although temperature and humidity might affect this.

High humidity will cause a dull finish, or what is sometimes called a polyamine blush. The finish, however, will hold and work just as well as if it had a high-gloss, glassy shine.

Reel Maintenance

R EEL CARE begins with how you use the reel. Use a reel properly, carefully, protect it from excessive exposure to water (especially salt water) and dirt and sand, and the reel will reward you with a long life and lots of fish.

"Protect it from excessive exposure to water" is not as silly as it first sounds. Many fishermen leave rigged rods in rod holders to and from the fishing grounds. This is typical on any larger boat that has a vertical, gunwale-mounted rod holder. Rough seas, however, can create constant spray that constantly soaks reels and rods.

Rods won't be hurt—they can be washed off—but this water could get inside a reel through the seams in side plates and fittings. Salt water is particularly damaging because the internal reel parts will start to corrode almost immediately. The salt water will also begin to break down any grease. This will start with exposed areas such as the levelwind worm gearing on casting and popping rods. Unfortunately, you won't see or feel this until the reel begins to go bad, so keep it inside a cabin or, if mounted on a rod, in protected racks during long runs.

Whenever you clean or check a reel, take it off the rod. It's not only easier to handle the reel this way, but the contact between the reel foot and the seat is eliminated. Corrosion and galvanic action can occur at this spot, and both will ruin the reel and the reel seat.

Storage

One of the common causes of reel damage, according to manufacturers, is improper storage. Broken bails and handles on spinning reels, broken levelwinds and handles on casting reels, and bent frames or spools on fly reels unfortunately

Reels that are not cared for can quickly become corroded, as shown by these two reel spools.

are not uncommon. Follow the tips in chapter 1 on general care for suggestions on proper reel storage.

Trip Checks

For want of a better term, I call these trip checks—done after each trip to be sure that everything is working properly. In essence they are nothing more than a quick look, a turn of the reel handle, an on/off check of the antireverse (spinning reels) or thumb bar/push button (casting reels), and spin of the drag before packing the reel for a trip or mounting it on a rod for fishing near my home. But you can check a lot in this, as follows:

1. Turn the handle a few times to check if the reel is working properly or if there are any binding, damaged or corroded ball-bearing drives, bent spools, broken levelwinds, and so on.
2. When turning the handle, flip the antireverse of spinning reels on and off a few times to make sure that it works properly and easily. When it is on, turn the reel handle backward to ensure the internal cog is grabbing the gear and preventing the reel handle from backturning.
3. Tighten the drag knob a turn or two and turn the spool on a spinning reel, or pull line from the reel on a fly, trolling, or casting reel. This will give you a rough, but immediate, indication of the drag performance and any binding, jerkiness, or erratic action.
4. Check the amount and condition of the line on the reel. The reel should be full and the line should be in good condition.
5. Push the push button or thumb bar of casting reels and pull lightly on the line to be certain the line release is working. Try the same thing after switching the flipping lever on those reels with this feature. This should place the reel in free spool when the thumb bar is depressed, and on drag when released. (In the casting mode, though, it will stay in free spool when released, and until the handle is turned.) Check other features of the reel now, too, because some casting and conventional reels have on/off clicks, antireverse switches, and so on.
6. Open and close the bail on spinning reels to make sure that this often-damaged part is freely working. Turn the handle at least once with the bail open to make sure that the trip mechanism closes the bail sharply.

It might seem as if this check and the regular check and cleaning listed below are the same, but they are not. This check can take less than a minute and requires no reel cleaning. In addition, this check prevents you from using a broken or nonfunctioning reel.

Two examples: On a recent airline trip I took four casting reels, which I packed in my luggage. At my destination, I used only two of the reels. When I returned home, I did not check or clean the reels that I had not used. Later, preparing for another trip and running through a trip check with those two unused reels, on one of them, I found that the shaft on which the levelwind runs had broken, making it inoperative. This probably occurred on the return airline trip, but I didn't notice it at the time.

After another trip I washed and cleaned a reel and stored it away, checking it at the same time. The next time I took it out and ran through the trip check, I immediately found that the main ball-bearing drive was frozen and corroded from salt water and that the reel handle would not even turn. That's the only time that this has occurred—probably because of hasty or improper cleaning, and the ball bearing corroded between the time of the washing/cleaning and the next trip.

Regular Checking and Cleaning Be very careful when choosing and using solvents. Many modern reels have plastic parts that can be damaged by organic solvents and cleaners. These include gasoline, acetone, carbon tetrachloride, kerosene, mineral spirits, and other canned or aerosol grease-cutting solutions.

I learned this lesson years ago when I dismantled a reel and dumped the entire contents into a small container of organic solvent. A few minutes later when I pulled the handle pad and the drag knob out, they were completely deformed. Many reels have slide plates, gears, levers, ratchets, drag knobs, and so on that can be ruined by the wrong solvent. Don't be fooled by appearance; many reel parts are plastics that have been plated or finished to look like metal.

To be safe, clean with a strong soapy solution, not a plastic-reacting solvent. When you want to determine if a part is metal or plastic, dip a cotton swab into the solvent and touch the part. If it then sticks, mattes the finish, softens the part, or does anything other than wipe on and off, do not use it. Even if it appears safe in this test, though, it may react during prolonged contact.

Another good cleaning method is to use Reel Scrubber. This 16-ounce aerosol solvent by Birchwood Casey Laboratories uses both high-powered propellent force and a strong solvent to remove dirt and grime without removing reel parts. Their tests so far show no problem with plastic parts of any reel, although it still pays to be careful and test a small area if unsure. It works well, although removal of strongly caked grease can be hastened with an old toothbrush working in conjunction with Reel Scrubber.

Use of Reel Scrubber, a pressurized reel solvent that will not harm reels, makes it easy to clean up a reel like this. On cases like this with old, built-up grease, a small brush in combination with Reel Scrubber works best and also reduces wasting of the solvent.

A good alternative to this is one of the computer and electronics micromolecular cleaners, such as Electro-Wash, which are used for cleaning circuit boards and other electronics. These products evaporate completely and clean thoroughly, but are best for light cleaning of reels and tackle parts.

Another solution is to use air pressure alone, such as the compressed air (like Dust-Off) available at most camera shops.

A Zebco spokesman suggests using a very diluted solution of nondetergent, organic soapy cleanser (such as Amway) to quickly break down the mineral deposits on the reels for a complete cleaning.

Reels will get dirty and require internal and external cleaning. Generally, internal cleaning and checking can be done annually. All reels have external parts, however, that can affect reel performance if they are not regularly cleaned. These include the line rollers on spinning-reel bails, the bail-pivoting mechanism that opens and closes the bail, the many parts on automatic one-hand-opening bails (in which a lever that raises as the line is picked up also opens the bail for instant casting), the front of the rear drag-control knob, handle parts, levelwind pawls, tracks on casting reels, various switches, levers, clicks, and other controls.

It is best to check and clean a reel after each fishing trip. Everybody seems to have different ideas on cleaning reels. Some like to use a garden hose, but most reel manufacturers specifically warn against this, probably because a hard spray could inject water into the reel. The high pressure caused by a nozzle can, theoretically, force water, dirt, and grime through the reel opening and side-plate flanges into the reel gearing, causing more problems than not cleaning.

If the reel was fished in salt water, the salt intrusion from such a hard spray could completely destroy the reel. In addition, a simple rinse or quick dip in fresh water will not remove the salt, only slightly dilute it for a moment.

The cleaning method that has worked well for me in both fresh and salt water includes the following:

1. Immediately after fishing, reduce the pressure on all drags. This will preserve the soft drag washers so that the drag will be functional the next time out.
2. Once home, remove the spools of those reels that allow easy removal. This includes spinning and most fly reels, and might even include some casting reels.
3. Fill a tub, dishpan, or sink with lukewarm water. Put the reels and spools into the water *briefly*—only enough to wet them.
4. Use a small scrub brush (an old toothbrush is ideal) to lightly scrub the reels, paying particular attention to small cracks and crevices, controls on the side plates, and so on. Do not allow the reels to soak a long time, because too much water can get into the reel. (Some water will get in, but this can occur to a slight degree when fishing also.)
5. Rinse the reels with clean fresh water, shake to throw off as much water as possible, dry as much as possible with a terrycloth towel. Place in an open area to air-dry, or use a hair dryer to dry the reels more rapidly.

This is really a two-part program, with the second procedure undertaken after the reels have completely air-dried. This includes lightly lubing and oiling external parts, as well as other protections. The best steps for this include:

1. After ensuring that the reel is completely dry, check all its working parts to be sure that it is properly functioning.
2. Referring to the reel's manual, lightly oil or grease each part indicated. This usually includes:

    A. Casting reels: Pawl or line-guide pin, worm or levelwind gear, left and right ball bearings, handle knob(s) and shaft, spool shaft ends, star drag control or levers. Dismantle the reel every few cleanings and grease the main, pinion, and cog gears. Take care with the leaf-spring-operated antireverse controls, because lubrication is seldom needed here—they are used so seldom—and excessive lubing can make them slip.

    B. Spinning reels: On the sides or under the rotating line roller, any rotating or lever bail arms or fittings, drag-knob nut and spring (front-drag reels), spool drag washers (but *only* if called for by the manufacturer because many reels' drags should be kept free of oil, grease, and water), antireverse lever or switch, handle nut, handle knob and shaft, and main shaft (underneath the removable spool).

    C. Spincast reels: Rotary pin (pickup pin) and spring (underneath the nose cone, which must be removed), handle knob and shaft, drag adjustment dial or star drag, antireverse lever, and main shaft (under spool).

    D. Single-action fly reels: Main shaft (remove spool) handle, drag lever or knob, internal drag controls, and spool-locking catch—if present.
3. If desired, and especially if fishing in salt water, consider spraying the reel lightly with a demoisturizing agent such as LPS #1, WD-40, CRC, or a similar solution. You might wish to cover the line or remove the spool so you won't spray the line. It won't hurt the line, according to line manufacturers, but might leave an odor. (This could be good or bad—some anglers use WD-40 on their lures as a scent to attract fish.)

Also check parts for wear. Wear is usually heavy on parts such as the levelwind pawl of casting reels and the roller on spinning reels. To check for easy rolling, run a piece of heavy line, string, or cord under the roller and slide it back and forth to check how freely it rolls.

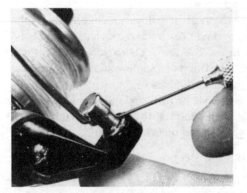

Using a needle-nose oiler to oil the roller on a spinning reel.

Chart of lube and oiling instructions for a variety of reels. These are Daiwa reels, but the basics would be the same for any reel. *Courtesy Daiwa.*

Baitcast Reels

1 Line guide pin
2 Worm shaft
3 Left and right ball bearing
4 Handle knob and shaft
5 Cog wheel
6 Both ends of spool shaft
7 Drive gear shaft (remove handle nut, plate screw and plate)
8 Pinion gear and spool shaft

Spincast Reels

1 Rotor pin and spring
2 Handle knob and shaft
3 Drag adjustment dial or star drag
4 Anti-reverse lever
5 Main shaft

Spinning Reels

1 Under Rotating line rollers
2 Arm lever and screw
3 Inside drag knob, nut and spring
4 Ball balance holder plate
5 Inside spool washers
6 Anti-reverse lever
7 Handle nut
8 Handle knob and shaft
9 Main shaft

Lube all screw threads and free them from corrosion

Baitcast Reels

1 Both ends of spool shaft
2 Left and right ball bearing
3 Drive gear — all surfaces
4 Drag washer — all surfaces
5 Pinion gear — all surfaces
6 Clutch lever and clutch stopper plate — on moving surface
7 Drive gear shaft
8 Star drag — on moving surface
9 Worm shaft — all surfaces
10 Line guide pin
11 Cog wheel shaft
12 Handle — knob and shaft

Spincast Reels

1 Drive gear — all surfaces and teeth
2 Pinion gear — spring and teeth
3 Drive gear shaft
4 Drag adjustment dial
5 Rotor pin and spring
6 Spool washer
7 Spool metal — all surfaces
8 Handle — knob and shaft
9 Anti-reverse cam

Spinning Reels

1 Inside drag knob, nut and spring
2 Inside spool washer — all surfaces
3 Mainshaft
4 Ball balance holder plate
5 Under rotating line rollers
6 Arm lever and screw — moving surfaces
7 Ball spring — all surfaces
8 Spool washer
9 Main shaft — all moving surfaces
10 Ratchet and screw
11 Ball bearing or bearing metal — all surfaces
12 Pinion gear — all surfaces
13 Oscillating gear and oscillating pinions — all surfaces
14 Drive gear teeth and shaft — all surfaces
15 Oscillating slider
16 Anti-reverse camshaft
17 Handle — knob and shaft

25

The levelwind pawls on casting reels are easily removed from a small cap on the underside of the levelwind housing. Remove the cap, pull out the pawl, clean off old grease, and check for wear. The working end of the pawl should have a small concave edge. If it is too thin from side to side, or reduced to a pinlike projection, it may cause binding, loosen the levelwind mechanism, or wear on the levelwind worm gear. Replace if necessary. (Most reels come with a small kit with spare levelwind pawls.)

Usually this regular check is enough to protect reels between annual checkups and lubes. The above might seem excessive, but it really does not take much time. The soak and quick scrub take no more than a few minutes for an average assortment of tackle, say four to six reels. The oiling takes a little longer once the reels are dry. How long will depend on whether you apply only external oil or internal oil, too. Oiling should not take more than a minute or two for each reel, and it will protect them. Make sure that when you are through, you back off the drag to protect the soft drag washers.

Annual Checks

Every extensively used reel should have an annual check, preferably at the end of the old season, not at the beginning of the new. You want to have time for repairs, which you won't if you wait until a day or two before you go fishing.

The annual check should be done after the washing outlined above. (You can skip oiling the reels, though, because it is part of the annual check.)

During an annual check you will strip the reel down to its basic parts, though not necessarily dismantling every single piece.

Basic tips for this annual check are:

1. Use a compartmented box such as a biscuit tin, egg carton, or plastic utility box to hold the parts. You will be partially disassembling the reel, so you need to keep the parts in order for easy reassembly. A handy tip here is to always work in one direction—left to right. That way the last item you took off will be in the box's farthest right-hand side, and will also be the first part that you put back on. You will never get mixed up.

2. Have all necessary tools ready. These include the reel tool that came with the reel, a set of small screwdrivers, and small wrenches. (For more details see chapter 10, on tools and equipment.)

3. Gather other cleaning materials. These can include old toothbrushes, pipe cleaners, small scrub brushes, old rags, cotton-tipped swabs, and so on that are used on large surfaces, in cracks, and around controls.

4. Make sure that you have the appropriate oil, grease, and demoisturizing agents. If possible, use the oil and grease recommended by the reel manufacturer. Do *not* use oil on gear parts or other reel areas where grease or a thick lubricant is suggested. A light oil here will run off and not protect. Do *not* use petroleum jelly, since it has poor adhesion and will not protect the gears as well as specifically recommended greases.

Some sort of compartmented box is best for dismantling reels, so that each part in turn can be placed in order in one of the compartments. This egg carton is ideal for this.

5. Keep a small pan of solvent nearby to clean parts when the reel is disassembled. *Do not* use organic solvents such as gasoline, carbon tetrachloride, acetone, or other highly flammable, dangerous, or unhealthy products. Gasoline is just plain dangerous to use, and carbon tet gives off toxic fumes. See note on cleaning and checking reels for details on solvents. Use soapy water or grease-cutting household cleaner to cut the grease, following directions on the bottle. Rinse thoroughly after cleaning each part. (Gasoline and organic degreasers, aside from the health and hazard dangers, will also leave a film on reel parts, which prevents proper molecular adhesion of any grease or oil.)

6. Dry the reel parts thoroughly after cleaning and rinsing, and before adding any oil or grease or reassembling. Air-drying is okay, but a hot-air hair dryer also works well. Make sure, though, that the forced air does not blow away any small or lightweight parts.

7. Work only on one reel at a time to avoid mixing parts.

Annual cleaning of reels follows the same procedure regardless of the type of reel, although the instructions for disassembly of each reel are different. The steps of cleaning and lubing should be as follows for all reels.

1. Disassemble the main parts of each reel. Work on only one reel at a time. How much disassembly is required will vary with the reel, how heavily you use it, and how comfortable you feel taking it apart (and putting it back together).

2. Once the major reel parts are disassembled, wash, clean, and examine them for wear or breakage. To clean the parts, take each in turn and scrub it carefully in the soapy, grease-cutting solution. Use an old rag or small scrub brush for the major parts, such a side plates and reel housings, and use a pipe cleaner or old toothbrush to clean around controls, levers, fittings, and other crevices that will harbor dirt and grime. If scrubbing a unit that holds smaller parts, do so with care to avoid dislodging any small loose parts. Or remove these small parts first, scrub thoroughly, and replace.

Most spinning reels have simple gearing that allows conversion of the rotary handle motion into the rotary bail movement (at right angles to the handle movement), along with an in-out reciprocating spool motion to help lay down the line. This reel has both a side plate and an end cap that must be removed.

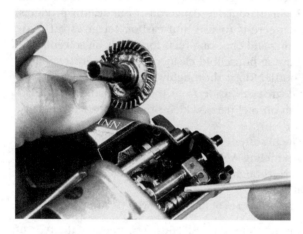

Removal of the main gear shows the gearing. The pointer shows a worm gear that gives the spool the reciprocating action.

Once all the grease and dirt are removed, rinse the parts several times and place on an absorbent terry towel or under a hair dryer to completely dry them.

3. Examine each part carefully. If a part is damaged or worn, you will have to repair or replace it (see chapter 7). If you are satisfied that the parts are clean and not worn, reassemble the reel, lubricating each part as you replace it.

Use only recommended grease on gears. These include pinion, main, cog wheels (gear), worm (levelwind gear on casting reels), spiral (on main shaft of spinning reels) and ratchet gears, levelwind pawl, and ends of spool shaft. Follow directions to lightly oil, if required, the drag washers, handle shafts, screws (to ease removal and reduce corrosion), spinning-bail rollers, star drag, spinning-reel main shafts, any controls, ratchets, springs, levers, and so on.

In most cases, fishermen add too much grease and oil. Apply *only* enough to cover the parts and coat the gears. There are two dangers in using too much grease or oil: Excessive grease or oil will hold dirt or grime into the reel, which will wear out the moving parts; and oil or grease will flow or migrate during warm weather and travel to other parts of the reel, where it may slow casting or interfere with a drag system.

Zebco tackle experts suggest applying oil with a dental pick or toothpick, which will ensure you use the right amount of lubrication and get it in the right spot. They also suggest applying grease with a toothpick to every two or three gear teeth on the main and pinion gears, so that it is properly distributed around the teeth. Some manuals suggest that you place a blob in only one spot so that the meshing of the gears will spread the grease. This does not always work as it should. Instead the grease is pushed to the outside flat area of the gear, where it does no good. A safer bet is to use Zebco's method.

Disassembling each type of reel is different, and each brand of reel will vary from other manufacturers' models. The following is a *general* guide. It should work well if you do not have your reel manual. If you do have your manual, follow it for detailed instructions.

Casting Reels Remove the right or handle side plate. In most reels this will remove a casing that holds all the gears in a side-plate housing. With the side plate removed, take out the spool. In older reels take care to not misplace the small brake blocks (centrifugal casting-control blocks) found on tiny shafts on the main spool shaft. To check the internal gears, you must remove the handle. To remove

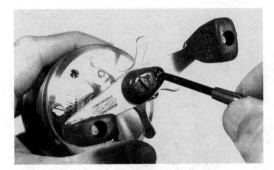

Checking a casting reel—step one—removal of the cap that covers the nut holding the handle in place.

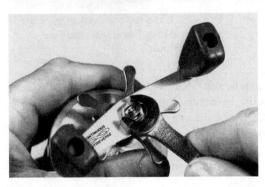

Checking a casting reel—step two—removal of the handle retaining nut.

Checking a casting reel—step three—removal of handle and handle washer.

Checking a casting reel—step four—removal of star drag (threaded—must be backed off).

Loosening screws (usually thumbscrews) removes the handle side plate from the reel body.

Centrifugal brake blocks on spindles on the reel spool (shown by pointer).

Removing screws that hold the external side plate to the base plate that holds the gearing and drag.

Side plate of the reel removed, showing the gearing and drag. The drag washers are on the handle shaft.

the handle, loosen and remove the handle nut. Most reels will have a small screw underneath this nut, which also must be taken out before the handle can be removed. To check the drag, back off the star drag to remove it and expose the flat and soft washers underneath that control drag pressure.

Additional screws in the side plate can be removed to expose the pinion (small) and main gears in the reel by which the handle turns the spool. Inspect it

30

The soft drag washer (left) rides in a recess on the main gear with the hard washer (raised).

Because they are open and in constant use when fishing, levelwinds on casting reels must be lubed frequently, usually daily. A long-nose tube of grease is needed to reach the worm gear.

On some casting reels, removing the screws will remove the cover on the left side plate.

Magnetic cast-control reels do not have centrifugal brake blocks, but instead use small magnets to create a magnetic field to control spool rotation.

all carefully. Loosen the screws on the left side plate to expose any gears and the spool shaft socket. Follow manual directions to remove the levelwind pawl (now more frequently called the line guide pin) and check for wear.

At this point, wash all parts as previously outlined, dry, oil, and grease as called for in the reel manual and reassemble.

Spinning Reels Remove the spool from the reel. Do not misplace any of the small, thin washers that are often on the shaft directly underneath (in back of) the spool. Take off the reel handle. Many spinning reels have both right- and left-hand drive, and the handles are removed in one of two ways. Hold the spool or engage the antireverse and turn the handle backward to loosen the screw shaft holding the reel, or remove the small screw on the opposite side of the shaft holding the reel body (the screw holds the shaft in place). When the screw is undone, slide out and remove the handle.

Remove the side plate. On most reels the left side plate is held on with several

Most reels today have convertible handles (convertible from right to left). The one on the left uses two different-sized threads to screw into the side of the reel shaft. Backing up the handle removes the handle. The center and right have straight-through shafts that are fastened in place with a cap on the side opposite the handle.

Parts of a simple spinning reel. Shown are the main reel body, handle, side plate, end cap, side-plate screws, gearing, and ball-bearing race.

(usually three) screws. Beneath the side plate you will see the reel's internal gearing, along with any rear drags, line slippage systems for bait fishing (these override the drag to allow line to pull from the spool with only light pressure), main shaft, antireverse systems and levers, and so on. In most cases, the main gear and drive (called pinion or planetary gear) are the only parts that will need attention.

If the grease on these parts is dirty, remove the pinion gear and wash it. Use a cleaning-solution-soaked toothbrush to clean the spiral gearing on the main shaft. Be careful not to dislodge any small parts that might be loose. If there are loose parts, remove them first, carefully noting their position and the settings on the reel. Occasionally, parts will not go back properly if a setting, such as an antireverse, is changed.

If the reel has a rear drag, drop some light oil on the drag washers, and turn it by turning the reel spool. Make sure that the drag is completely backed off to allow for maximum penetration of the lubricant. Also lube the handle, bail, handle shaft, and so on as previously outlined.

Fly Reels Single-action fly reels, which are used most widely and uniformly in both fresh- and saltwater fishing, are simple spool-and-frame devices. Even the

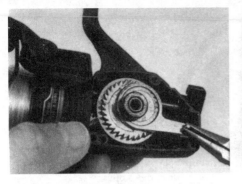

Removing the pin on a reel. This pin holds the cam lever into the reel spool shaft, causing the reciprocating action of the spool while turning the handle. Often removal of some part like this is necessary to get the gears out and exposed, although all reels are slightly different.

Gearing of the above reel, with pin in place to show position; cam lever removed.

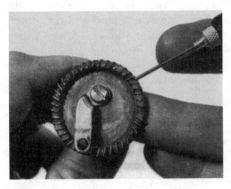

Gears in all reels *must* be lubricated by depositing a drop of oil or grease on each gear tooth. You cannot deposit the grease or oil in one spot and count on the turning gears to distribute the lubrication.

Gearing and controls in some reels are more complicated than in others. This reel has all the typical gearing, with a rear bait-release drag system (in addition to the standard front spool drag).

most expensive and exotic fly reels, such as the Fin-Nor, are made of only a few simple parts that are easily disassembled and maintained.

First remove the reel's spool. On many reels a small button or spring lever releases the spool from a catch on the main shaft. Once the spool is removed, check the clicks and drag mechanism on the inside of the frame. Drags will vary with fly reels, ranging from the larger brake disc, such as on the Fin-Nor and other specialty saltwater models, to smaller lever-tension devices found on smaller reels.

Cleaning and lubing are easy because these reels are open and simple. Just removing the spool usually makes it possible to scrub and clean the inner reel frame and the spool. Light lubing on all moving parts is also easy and all that is required for most fly reels.

Spincast Reels Spincast reels are generally easy to clean and lube. On many of

Fly reel with the spool removed, showing the simple pawls and drag systems used on most of these reels.

them, removing the nose cone releases the inner gearing and spool for cleaning, examination, and lubing. Other spincast reels have a removable side plate or side-plate screws that release the inner gearing and controls. Once these are exposed, examine them carefully.

Since spincast reels are enclosed in a protective one-piece housing only opened through the removal of the overlapping nose cone, they generally stay clean. The exception can come from poor handling when sand and dirt enter through the push-button control or drag setting. Clean and lube as above, using grease on the gears. Greasing properly here is equally as important as on spinning reels, so use the proper grease and the toothpick application method mentioned above for general cleaning and lubing. Replace the gears in the main housing, and reassemble by replacing the nose cone.

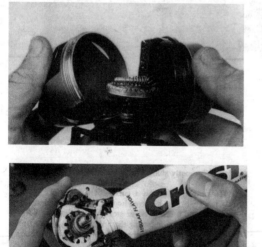

Removal of cone from spincast reel often allows opening of the reel cavity and simple gearing. This makes lubrication and repairs simple.

A good trick to make gearing on new reels smoother is to apply toothpaste. This should be done *only* if the reel is new (use will have smoothed the gears out already) and if the gearing is high-quality brass or stainless steel. If the reel has cast- or pot-metal parts or nylon gears, this procedure may ruin the gearing. The toothpaste is packed in the gear housing of the reel (casting or spinning) and the reel handle turned to "lap" the gearing. The toothpaste must be removed with water and the reel regreased before use.

Lure Maintenance

W HERE YOU DRAW the line between lure maintenance and lure repair is imprecise and somewhat subjective. Check chapter 8, Lure Repair, for additional help and suggestions.

Lures might not seem to require maintenance or special care, but they do. While lures don't require lubing like reels, or guide checks to prevent line damage, they can and do become damaged if not handled properly. Lures can also damage other lures or tackle. A prime example is keeping soft-plastic lures with hard lures in the same tacklebox tray over a winter, only to find a sticky, gooey mess come spring.

As with the chapter on lure repair, each type of maintenance procedure will be covered.

Sharpening Hooks

This is listed first because of its prime importance. A lure lacking an absolutely sharp hook is not as effective as it should be for fishing. With the possible exception of chemically sharpened hooks, no hook is as sharp out of the box as it should be. This applies especially to lure hooks.

Banging around in a tacklebox, scraping against a boat, hitting a snag, knocking against a rock, scraping a barnacle or oyster bed, hooking into a duck-blind piling, in short, anything that a hook comes in contact with will dull it. This includes hooked fish, especially those species with hard, bony mouths.

How to properly sharpen a hook is based on its style.

1. To properly sharpen a curve-point hook (like the Eagle Claw–style), use a curved hook hone to work on the curve's inside and a flat hone or stone on its outside. Work in a curved motion, following the hook's shape, and move from the barb to the end of the point. Use lighter pressure at the point end to avoid rounding and dulling it.

2. For straight points, use a hone to triangulate the point, again working from the barb to the point. To triangulate the point, work with a file, hone, or stone at an angle on the hook's inside, working first on one side and then the other, so that you form a slight knife or wedge edge on the inside from the point to the barb. This is easy to follow because most hooks have a

dark finish (japanned, bronze, or black), and the sharpened point will become shiny as the coating is removed. To complete the triangle, concentrate on the flat outside of the point, working across it to make one flat side and two more wedge edges.

The result is a point that has three flat sides and three flat edges that form a cutting-edge triangle in cross section. When sharpening the point this way, do not weaken the point by removing too much metal. This method is ideal for any hook point—no matter what the size.

3. Hooks can also be triangulated with the flat surface in the *inside* of the hook point and the two angled cutting edges on its *outside*. Just reverse the sharpening methods mentioned above. I feel that on some hooks this removes a little more metal in the point area, which may weaken the hook somewhat. It is far easier to work angle cuts on the outside of the hook point, however, rather than on the inside, where the file or hone must run between the shank and the point. This is a good method for flies, bugs, and grubs that could be damaged if hit with the file.

4. Another method for sharpening straight-point hooks is to use a diamond shaping. The only difference here is that the hook point is finished by making two more angular sharpening motions on the outside of the hook point in the point and barb area.

The result from the two cuts on the hook's inside and two on the outside is a point that will have a diamond-shaped cross section instead of a triangle form. The only danger in using this method is on small hooks, because it might remove too much metal and weaken the hook point and barb area. For larger hooks it is ideal, since it provides four cutting edges and four flat sides that offer good cutting and hook penetration.

The problem with sharpening is that as soon as the hooks are honed, they can quickly become dulled by rattling around in a tacklebox. Yet there is a real advantage to sharpening hooks at home or during the off season, since you don't want to spend all your fishing time sharpening hooks. One way to do this, yet still protect the hooks, is to sharpen them at home (there are several electric or battery-operated hook sharpeners available to make this easy), and then add hook guards.

There are several ways to maintain sharp hook points. One is to lay hooks in a row between two strips of masking tape, but this can get messy. If the tape gets old, it is also difficult to remove. Another method is to save old torn-up plastic worms to use as a protective sheath on the hooks. Once all your hooks are sharpened, use a low heat to melt down the old worms (color won't matter) and, when liquid, dip each hook into the molten plastisol to cover it with a protective soft-plastic coating. When fishing, it takes only a second to rub off this protective coating.

Sharpeners must be chosen according to hook size and style. There are a number of hook sharpeners on the market, ranging from small rectangular, triangular, and rounded stones; diamond hook hones; and electric hook hones, such as the battery-operated Berkley Line Stripper (which has a hone on its end), and the

Pocket Hook Sharpener and Power Stone (both battery operated), by JWA. I like a small half-round cross section, D-shaped hook hone (the Ocean Pointer) by Diamond Machining Technology for field and boat use. Other diamond hook hones such as the small pen-type hone from Gaines and the several grits (fine, medium, and coarse, depending upon the size of the hook) from Eze-Lap are also excellent.

Larger hooks, such as those used for offshore fishing, often require a file. Good files include those made by Red Devil and Nicholson Rotary Mower Files, and the smaller files from Luhr Jensen, the West Coast tackle company. Any file will rust rapidly. To prevent this, make a sheath for the file and keep it well soaked with WD-40. A sheath can be made from a fancy leather or nothing more than a stiff plastic bag, folded and taped to hold the file.

Lure Storage

Proper lure storage is probably the second most important concern in lure maintenance, because as previously mentioned, mixing lures of different materials can ruin lures. The main problem is mixing soft and hard lures. Soft plastics are made of a plastisol that will attack harder plastics. At one time this was a problem with tackleboxes, because the then-new plastic worms would soften, melt, and erode the box trays. Manufacturers have since wormproofed boxes by using materials such as polypropylene that resist attack by most lures. Avoid using other boxes for lure storage, such as lightweight plastic utility boxes, or old tackleboxes, because they may erode. If you have an old pre-wormproof box, you can still use it, but keep all the worms in plastic bags.

When soft-plastic worms and other lures come in contact with each other, the worms melt and the lures' finish is damaged. This chemical reaction will affect molded-plastic lures, painted finishes, plastic and rubber skirts, such as those on spinner- and buzzbaits, and enameled jig heads. They won't attack metal-plated lures, though softened plastic will stick to and ruin metal spoons and spinners.

Contact between soft-plastic lures and spinnerbaits, and buzzbaits and similar skirts and rubber tails, be they plastic or vinyl, are equally damaging, causing these parts of both lures to react and melt.

The degree of reaction and damage depends upon the type of soft plastic. All soft-plastic lures are made of a plasticizer, or softener, which makes the lure soft, and a plastisol, a hardener. The degree of softness or hardness of a lure is based strictly on the ratio of the softener to the hardener. Color dye or pigments are also added, along with (occasionally) scents, salt, and other chemicals.

Harder baits, such as those used in salt water for grubs, plastic trolling lures, trolling eels, and so on are harder and less reactive. The soft-plastic lures, however, have more plasticizer in them, which makes them more slippery, and they are more likely to release this liquid when in contact with another lure or when heated to high temperatures. Some manufacturers take pains to prevent this interaction.

Some lures have a hard body into which a soft-plastic tail is inserted. This is done in order to make the soft-plastic tail replaceable. The hooking arrangement is in the hard-bait body—not in the soft-plastic tail. In most cases, a special type of paint is used so that the soft-plastic tail and hard-plastic body don't chemically react with each other.

Other companies have similar protection for their lures. Most of these are more durable, soft lure-resistant finishes, according to several lure manufacturers, which are epoxy instead of the urethane and lacquer finishes normally used. The epoxies are two-part paints, making them harder to mix and requiring longer drying times than the urethanes, all of which makes production time slower. Most companies at the present do not seem to like epoxies and do not generally use them.

Vinyl lures are less likely to react with hard baits. These lures and teasers consist of hard plastic heads with vinyl skirts. They are seldom carried in tackleboxes with other lures because of their size, and are more typically stored separately in a rolled-up lure bag.

Soft lures will generally not attack each other, but avoid mixing different brands that might use different plastics. When different colors of soft lures are mixed together, the colors may bleed. The darker color usually bleeds into the lighter or translucent lures. This won't be a noticeable problem if you keep black, grape, and blue plastic worms together; it will be a problem if you mix black with translucent yellow. Fluorescent colors will also bleed into each other.

Bleeding, reacting with other lures, and melting are all exacerbated with heat. Some soft-plastic lure companies have tested lures in closed tackleboxes with temperatures of over 200°F. This caused the softener of the soft-plastic lures (the plasticizer) to leak out of the lure. Even if the plasticizer does not attack another lure's finish, it will leave a gummy coating. To prevent this, keep tackleboxes out of the heat or cover with a wet towel when fishing.

Ironically, in some tests by outdoor writer Lefty Kreh, heat buildup does not seem to be affected by a tacklebox's color. Lefty drilled a hole in several boxes so he could glue in dial thermometers to check temperatures in brown and white tackleboxes left in the sun during August. There was no appreciable temperature difference, so be sure to keep your boxes out of the heat.

All rubber skirts eventually break down in time and will mat with and attack the finish of hard lures. This is more frequent with natural rubber skirts than with vinyl or plastic skirts. It is also more prevalent when the lures are exposed to sun, which happens with any of the clear- or translucent-top satchel-type tackleboxes, because UV rays penetrate the box. To prevent this, keep the skirts in a separate box, keep the tacklebox out of the sun, or cover it with a towel. Keep all skirted lures apart from other lures.

In addition to separate storage, there are ways to keep rubber skirts so that their action is still what it should be when the lure is fished. Several experts and lure manufacturers suggest storing skirts in a bottle of pork rind, which keeps the rubber flexible and prevents matting. You can use a freshwater-filled old pork-rind jar, baby food jar, or plastic screw-lid food jar for the same purpose. ArmorAll will help to clean and free stuck skirts.

Another possibility is to remove skirts and store them in cornmeal, cornstarch, or talcum powder. All will keep skirts from sticking and matting. Also, carefully examine lures periodically and replace skirts where necessary.

The best solution of all is to be aware of the potential problems and avoid mixing lures. Some suggestions include:

1. Store different lures in separate compartments. Especially important is keeping hard lures, spinnerbaits, buzzbaits, jigs, spoons, and soft-plastic lures separated.
2. To prevent soft-plastic lure colors from bleeding into other soft lures, store different colors in separate tacklebox compartments or use lightweight sandwich bags to hold different brands and colors of soft plastics.
3. To keep spinnerbaits and buzzbaits from melting, store them in the spinnerbait compartments in some tackleboxes, in a bottle of water (or pork rind), or in cornmeal or cornstarch.

Rusted hooks and lures become a problem when they are poorly stored. Hooks in particular are damaged by excessive moisture trapped in a closed tacklebox. Plated spoons, metal lips, and bills on crankbaits, spinners, spinnerbaits, and buzzbaits are less subject to damage because of the nickel or chrome plating. Avoiding rust problems begins when you're fishing. Shake lures to remove any excess water before putting them back in a tacklebox, and do not leave a tacklebox open during a rain drizzle or where or when it could be hit by boat spray.

One easy solution to this when boat fishing is to mount lure holders on the boat. At the beginning of each trip, pick out the lures you think you might use and place them in the lure rack. (Even if you use more lures during the day, this gives you a head start.) Keep the lures in the rack until the end of the day, or even after you trailer the boat home, when you can properly dry them before replacing them in the tacklebox. Often just the air-drying on a trailer trip is enough to remove most of the moisture. If lures are not thoroughly dry when you put them back in the tacklebox, leave the tacklebox open to allow the moisture to escape and the box to breathe.

Saltwater lures present problems. These are primarily caused by the leaders used with offshore trolling lures and by the size of many lures. Large lures should be kept in large-compartment tackleboxes that are expressly made for their storage. Satchel-type boxes come with compartment dividers, but the dividers do not have to be used. Instead, individually fit large lures in the compartments. Saltwater trolling lures used for billfish, wahoo, dolphinfish, and so on are large, have vinyl skirts and are usually built on leaders ranging from 6 to 20 feet long. These won't fit in a tacklebox but should be stored. You can use one of the popular soft lure caddies that feature clear vinyl pockets (the better to see and select lures) in an apron that can be fastened on a boat with hook-and-loop fasteners, Velcro, grommets, or snaps. The large pockets make it possible to roll up the leader with the lure for storage, while the apron can be taken down and rolled.

Other large-lure storage methods include built-in-the-boat lockers and large-diameter lure tubes, which are similar in principle to 35mm film canisters.

Washing Lures

Lures can become dirty, especially when you've been fishing in dirty, stained, muddy, alga-filled, or polluted water. To protect lures and restore their finish, wash them off at home. To do this, soak them in warm water, and scrub with a small stiff-bristle brush. An old toothbrush is ideal for this. A little liquid soap helps, particularly if the lures are coated with algae, slime, or dirt.

Once clean, rinse the lure thoroughly, set it on a draining board or hang on a lure rack, and allow it to dry before replacing it in the tacklebox.

Saltwater lures, in particular, should be washed, because the corrosive effects of salt water on hooks and metal are far more damaging than fresh water. Again, the solution is to soak, wash, and rinse in fresh water.

One word of advice on washing lures. Do not boil them or place in any hot liquid. According to a major manufacturer, an angler tried this with about 40 dirty lures. The result was—and will be—lures that were deformed, split, and swollen, just like the adverse reaction that can occur from excessive heat in a tacklebox.

Another word of advice. Consider removing hooks if you are scrubbing them very hard or you are working with many lures. Otherwise use extreme care in washing them to avoid injury.

Tuning Lures

Whether tuning is repair or maintenance is anyone's guess, but I consider it more maintenance because it involves adjustment.

Some simple tuning methods for various lures are as follows:

Crankbaits If crankbaits lack a line tie—split or jump ring, line connector, Duo-Lock snap, and so on—add one. This is particularly important for maximum action of the lure, and especially when heavy-pound-test line, which limits lure action when tied directly to a lure, is used.

Lures can become bent or damaged so that they will not run true. There are two ways to correct this. One is to bend the line-tie eye to rebalance the lure. Hold the lure with the eye facing you and use pliers to just slightly bend the eye in the direction opposite to which it runs. (If the lure runs to your right on retrieve, hold the lure with the eye toward you and bend the eye slightly to the left.) Check the retrieve and rebend until the lure runs straight.

You can also shave the side of the lip on plastic-lip lures. Again hold the lure with the eye toward you and shave the side opposite that of which the lure runs. Check the retrieve and repeat until satisfied with a straight retrieve.

Spinnerbaits Make sure that the wires are straight, the blades free, and the skirt unmatted. If the right-angle wiring bends when landing a fish, re-form it to the original position for proper action.

Buzzbaits Buzzbaits must also have straight wires, although some are designed so that they will work better if the wire is slightly bent down so that the lure and

One way to tune a lure to make it run straight is to scrape the side of the plastic lip as shown. To make the lure run true, always scrape the side opposite the way the lure runs. Thus, with this lure running to the left of you on retrieve, scrape the right side as you hold the lure with the head facing you (as in this photo).

hook ride lower in the water. For maximum action and noise, bend the upper arm down slightly so that the propeller blade will just tick against the lower arm as the blade turns.

Worms Make sure that the worm is rigged on a straight hook for maximum natural action in the water. If not, remove the hook and start over. (An exception is bending or twisting the worm to make a "swimming worm.")

Spoons Use an eye ring or snap for maximum action and to prevent the line from cutting off with the stamped ring on most spoons.

Removing Lure Dressings

Lure scents are tremendously popular today, with dozens of companies offering various aromas for almost every fish. Included are scents for largemouth bass, smallmouth bass, crappies, trout, salmon, catfish, carp, walleyes, saltwater species, and so on.

Some lures are even designed to hold scents with flocked surfaces (spinnerbait heads, jig heads, bullet worm weights), flocked materials (jig collars, flocked beads and bubbles), and special spongelike scent holders that fit into scent compartments. In many cases, however, and particularly with soft lures such as worms, scents will harm the lure if they are allowed to remain. For example, when scents first appeared, many bass pros soaked their worms in them for days before a fishing trip or tournament. The result was often ruined, gummy, or melted lures.

To avoid this, yet to still take advantage of the scents, soak lures only for a day and soak only those lures you know you will be using. Scents can be washed off lures after a trip to prevent damage. Scents are water or oil based, but soapy water will clean either.

Component Attachment

Many plugs or crankbaits come with wobbling plates, lips and bills, hook hangers, and so on, which are attached with screw eyes and small screws. In time, these can loosen, and you can lose hooks and fish. To prevent this, check lures annually to see if eyes and screws are secure.

Use a small screwdriver, like the one in your rod/reel repair kit (see chapter 10 on tools and equipment), to refasten screws, and use small needle-nose pliers to turn screw eyes farther into the lure. If screws and screw eyes seem excessively loose, remove them, apply a small amount of epoxy or instant glue into the hole, and quickly reinsert the screw or screw eye. A straight pin or straightened paper clip works well to get the glue into the hole.

It's also worth gluing eyes and screws into lures when fishing for larger-than-normal fish, because the eye or hanger is more secure. Another safety device consists of running a short length of wire or monofilament leader from the tail hook eye, through the belly hook eye, then fastening it to the lure's split-ring line tie or forward screw eye. Crimping sleeves work well to hold these in place with minimum interference with the lure. The result holds large toothy fish when a lure might break during the fight or be splintered on the strike. It is not necessary on saltwater plugs that feature through-wire construction for hanging hooks or use a plate insert as hook hangers.

For information on hook and part replacement and repainting, rubber coating, dyeing, polishing, re-forming, remelting, gluing, refinishing, and rerigging lures, see chapter 8, Lure Repair.

Accessory
Maintenance

A CCESSORIES REQUIRE CARE and maintenance. Failure to do so can result in the greater expense incurred replacing them, the real chance of lost fish when nets and gaffs fail, and the frustration of having pliers that won't work and knives that won't cut when you need them.

Spooling Line

Line must be spooled properly on reels to prevent twist, tangles, and other problems. Most line problems are caused by improper line spooling, using lures without adequate swivels so line twists, or turning the reel handle without retrieving line (as when snagged, fighting a fish resisting drag, taking out line, and so on).

Monofilament line has a characteristic called memory, which means that it will "set" in the position that it has when spooled on a service spool or spool filled for resale. For best line performance, fill the spool so that the line goes on the reel in the same way that it comes off the spool. There are several ways to do this, as follows:

1. On any revolving-spool reel (such as a casting, conventional surf, boat, or offshore trolling reel), run the line end through the levelwind (on casting reels) or line guard (fly reels) and tie with a simple overhand knot around the reel spool arbor. Maintain tension and spool the line on the reel with the spool turning in the same direction as the reel spool.
2. For spinning reels, there are two schools of thought. Traditionally, it was thought that spinning line should be spooled on a reel off the end of the spool, again going in the same direction. In doing this, the line comes off the side of the spool. Spool diameters vary widely (a 100-yard spool might measure 4 or 5 inches), so it is often necessary to turn the spool over during the spooling to prevent twisting.

   To check for twisting when spooling the line, periodically relax the tension on the line between the reel and manufacturer's spool. If it twists, turn the spool over and continue, checking again after about 15 to 20 turns of the reel handle. This may have to be done several times when spooling large reels, especially if using large-diameter service spools.

A standard method for spooling line is to spool spinning line off the end of the spool and casting line off the side of the spool. This prevents twist problems.

The second method of spooling line comes from research done by Berkley when they introduced a new line and spool packaging. They found that spool position or alignment makes no difference in line spooling. Their packaging is made so that the line spool can be hung on the rod in front of the butt guide and spooled directly onto the reel. They discovered that even though the line is coming off a revolving spool and being spiraled onto the end of a spool, it seemed to make no difference in fishing performance.

Proper tension is a must when spooling line. Too much tension will pack line on too tightly; no or too little tension might leave loops or looseness in the line. The best way to spool line is to mount the reel on the rod, run the line through the butt guide of the rod, and use a fishing towel or old rag to maintain tension as the line is spooled on. Turn the reel handle with your reel hand while using the other hand to control the line tension.

Line Care

Line care is simple but differs depending on the type of line. Fishing lines include monofilament typically used for all spinning and much casting, surf, and offshore fishing; braided Dacron and the new gel-spun fiber lines, used for some casting and offshore trolling; wire used for deep inshore trolling, lead-core line, also used for deep inshore trolling; and fly lines. Each of these will be covered in turn.

Monofilament Line manufacturers report that nothing short of battery acid will hurt monofilaments. Insect repellents, suntan lotions, sunblocks, perfume, deodorants, aftershave lotions, oil, grease, demoisturizers, gasoline, cologne, fly-line cleaners and dressings, leader sinks, baits, scent lotions and gels, chum, and so on will not harm monofilaments. They might impart a smell that could repel fish, but neither the tensile and knot strength nor any other critical property of the line will be damaged. Oil or grease will not harm line, but they will pick up dust and dirt that will abrade the line and the rod guides in time.

Basic monofilament care involves keeping the line twist-free and clean. To keep twist out, spool line properly on the reel and fish with care. Lures that turn in one direction, such as spinners, will impart twist to any line. When fishing these lures, use a keel, several good ball-bearing swivels, or change lures periodically to reduce twist. Twist can be taken out by removing the lure from the end of the line and trailing it in a current or behind a moving boat for several minutes.

Twist can also occur by cranking the reel handle on spinning reels when the drag slips. If the drag slips, it means that the line is not coming in and that each turn of the spinning-reel spool is putting one turn of twist into the line.

Abrasion will damage and weaken line. Line fished around obstructions should be checked and cut back a few feet at a time throughout the day to prevent breakoffs.

Braided Dacron Braided Dacron is ideal for revolving-spool reels when fishing in open water or when the least amount of stretch is desired. Care in using Dacron involves splicing the line (see instructions that come with the line for loop and line-to-line instructions) or using specific knots to prevent breakage. It does not have good knot strength when using the same knots that are popular for monofilament.

Gel-spun fiber lines and their related thermal-treated lines are ideal for casting and spinning (thermal). They are very thin in diameter when compared to monofilament of equal strength and have even less stretch than Dacron. Thus, they are ideal for bait and supersensitive fishing. They do require special knots.

Wire Single-strand wire is used inshore in salt water and in freshwater lakes for deep-water trolling, often for trout or cold-water species that travel open water in or near thermocline levels. You must prevent wire from kinking or bending. Kinks must be either replaced or repaired with a line-twisted splice of the two broken ends (almost like a haywire twist) and finished with a tight wrap. To avoid kinks and bends, it is necessary to control the line—never free-spool it without control over the spool. Lack of control when setting out lines results in overruns and kinks.

Lead-Core Trolling Line This is more forgiving than single-strand wire, because a break in the lead does not mean that the line will break. This line is made of a lead core covered with braided nylon. This covering is usually about 40-pound test. It still requires care, however, to avoid sharp bends and breaks.

Fly Lines Fly lines come in a variety of styles, sizes, and types, including floating and sinking (several sink-rate lines); level, double-taper, and weight-forward; shooting and running lines, specialty intermediate floating, sinking-tip lines, and so on. Most of these, however, are made of a PVC coating over a braided nylon core, and require different care than the lines previously covered.

Fly lines can be harmed by chlorinated solvents, which include products such as gasoline, insect repellents, and suntan lotions. Avoid them and either apply products, such as suntan lotion or insect repellents, with the back of your hand, or wash your hands after application to prevent damaging your fly line.

Pliers and Crimping Tools

Pliers, along with related tools like crimpers, seem almost indestructible, but they do require care. For example, pliers can rust and the joint can bind up from rust or saltwater corrosion. To prevent problems, regularly clean pliers in soapy water, dry completely, and spray liberally with a demoisturizing agent such as WD-40. Do not keep them in a holster after a trip (especially salt water), because this will prevent the pliers from drying out. If used in salt water, rinse with fresh water, then spray with WD-40.

If pliers do get tight or bound up, there are several remedies. One is to open and close them several times while sprinkling them with a powdered kitchen cleanser. The cleanser will act as a mild abrasive to polish the joint and make it work freely again. Rinse between each time. Then dry and spray as above.

Another solution is to spray pliers liberally with WD-40 or Liquid Wrench and let them soak overnight. This will usually release rusted or corroded pliers.

Line Clippers

Line clippers are not wire clippers. Use them for monofilament and nothing else and they will last a long time. Cutting wire or anything else will damage cutting jaws, rendering them useless for cutting line. Keep them clean, and rinse with WD-40 between trips.

Fillet, Bait, and Other Knives

Keep knives sheathed when not in use and keep them sharp at all times. To sharpen any knife, use a good sharpening stone, coat liberally with oil, and run the knife across it as if trying to "cut" the stone while holding the blade at about a 10° to 15° angle. Use the shallower angle for fillet and sharp slicing blades; the wider angle for blades used for bait cutting, chopping, and coarse knife work.

Rules and Bumping Boards

Keep rules and bumping boards clean and where they will not get scratched or the numbers defaced. Most anglers keep the engraved or stamped aluminum or plastic bumping board in the live well of the boat, where it is ready to use and protected from damage.

Sharpening Stones and Hook Sharpeners

Keep sharpening stones for hooks and knives separate because the hooks will often groove a stone in time, and a grooved stone will not effectively sharpen a knife. To keep stones from filling with steel filings from the sharpening process, float them with oil before using them.

Nets

In this age of nylon-net bags there is no longer the problem with mildew and rot that there was with bags of other materials. Bags should be washed regularly and dried, however, before storing.

Gaffs

Gaffs should be kept sharp, using the same methods of triangulating the hook as a fishhook (see chapter 4, Lure Maintenance). To keep gaffs either from being damaged or damaging other things (including anglers), store them properly in gaff holders or racks under the gunwale of the boat.

Rod Cases and Bags and Reel Cases

To keep the threads on better aluminum rod cases working smoothly, touch them occasionally with candle wax or spray them lightly with WD-40.

Keep rod bags dry and clean. If they get dirty, wash and dry them before using. Do not store wet rods in rod bags, particularly if the bagged rod is going into a case. If you must put a wet rod in a bag, leave it out to dry completely before storing it in a case.

Use the same care with reel cases as outlined with rod bags.

Ice-Fishing Tools

Spray with a demoisturizer, such as WD-40, after the season to keep all metal tools—ice spuds, ice skimmers, and so on—in good condition.

Waders and Hip Boots

There are two schools of thought on caring for waders and hip boots. First, most anglers agree that the major problem comes from rubber or rubberized canvas/nylon, not neoprene. Rubber can break down in time, primarily from stress (wrinkles, folds, stretching, and so on) and from ozone, an oxygen radical (O_3) that will destroy rubber. Ozone is formed naturally in the air, but is also actively discharged by electric motors. For starters, don't store any boots or waders near any electric motors.

Of the two schools of thought, one suggests folding hip boots and waders, storing them in a sealed plastic bag, and, if possible, removing air from the bag with a vacuum cleaner. Then store the bag in a box and store in a cool, dry, dark area.

A cool, dry, and dark area is also suggested for the second storage method, which is nothing more than hanging the boots or waders upside down from boot hangers. The best hangers for this purpose seem to be those that grip the boots right above the heel and hold them securely without gripping or touching the upper, more flexible, and thinner part of the boot.

Boots *must* be completely dry before storage. You can allow them to air out after a trip by folding them inside out (or inside out as far as possible for boot-foot waders). Special air-dryers such as electric boot heaters, and even a hair dryer stuck down a boot, will hasten this. Don't assume that the boots are dry just because you did not fall in the water. Perspiration also moistens the inside of boots and will lead to early dry rot and fabric breakdown if not removed.

Tackleboxes

Tacklebox problems result from abuse. A Plano spokesman notes that tackleboxes are typically overfilled by fishermen, who try to stuff 10 pounds of lures into a box designed to hold 5 pounds. This results in stressed and broken hinges, cracked lids (especially on satchel-type boxes), and damaged or broken latches. The commonsense solution is to buy another box for the other 5 pounds of gear.

Tackleboxes loose in a boat can cause problems for both the boxes and other tackle. Three of my satchel boxes weigh between 9½ and 10½ pounds each, and they would be heavier if I carried metal spoons or jigs. Tackleboxes will bang around the deck of a boat in rough water and, regardless of the manufacturer or construction, they just can't take that abuse. Lids will crack, as will boxes. Common sense dictates using a special hook-and-loop (such as Velcro) fastener or elastic (bungee) cord to hold boxes in place when running.

A third problem involves too much heat, a point also emphasized by lure manufacturers. Too much heat can result from a hot day or from storing a box in a closed car. The result can be temperatures in the box that, according to some reports, approach 300° F. At that temperature, soft lures will leak their elasticizer into puddles in the box, and hard lures can deform, split, and even blow up.

Damage is caused by the excessive heat, which is close to the temperature of the plastic when it is made by injection molding, along with a gas that develops from soft-plastic lures and expanded air or gas in the hard lures. This is not the fault of the tacklebox, because this will occur at the same temperatures and conditions whether the tackle is in or out of the box. The result is messy plastic puddles in lure compartments, puddles of plasticizer on hard plugs if they leak from one compartment to another, and UV penetration through the box's clear lids, which damages soft-plastic lures and rubber skirts. The gas that can build up can cause a slight warpage of the box, lids, and compartment sides according to tacklebox manufacturers.

The solution when fishing in the heat is to use a box with an opaque lid (which prevents UV rays from penetrating the box) or to cover the box with a light-colored towel. When it is very hot, wet the towel so that evaporation will help cool the box. You can also open the box slightly to prevent buildup of pressure or damaging gas.

Another problem, according to some, is the potential for different chemical interactions by lures stored in the boxes. "Chemicals have been added to this sport," one tackle rep notes. The combinations of worm hardeners and softeners; colors, salts, and scents added to soft-plastic lures and worms; the varying contents of worms from overseas; and the homebrews made by do-it-yourselfers can result in effects that are impossible to predict. Again, the commonsense solution is to keep worms in sealed plastic bags within the tacklebox.

Depthfinders

Depthfinders are beyond the scope of this book, but help is available from several manufacturers. If you own a Humminbird depthfinder, write for the specific owner's manual of your unit, c/o Techsonic Industries, No. 3 Humminbird Lane, Eufala, AL 36027 (800-633-1468). Lowrance Electronics provides similar information in the back of the owner's manual supplied with each unit. Information can also be obtained by calling their customer service department (800-324-1356) or writing to Lowrance Electronics, Inc., 12,000 East Skelly Drive, Tulsa, OK 74128. Similar help from Eagle is available by calling 800-324-1354 or by writing to Eagle Electronics, Inc., Box 669, Catoosa, OK 74015.

CHAPTER

Rod Repair

RODS CAN EASILY be repaired by most anglers because the principles are simple, the work is easy, and the tools and materials required are minimal. Rod repair can include anything from replacing a guide, to fixing a loose reel seat, to rebuilding a damaged cork grip, to even repairing a broken rod section.

Whether rods are factory or custom-made, they are assembled from parts, with the butt cap, grips, and reel seat all mounted and glued in place on the rod blank; the guides wrapped in place with thread.

Each part will be discussed in turn with the repair problems encountered and their solution or solutions.

Butt Caps

Butt caps are made of rubber or plastic and are usually found on any rod with straight-through construction. This rod is built with the rod blank extending through the handle instead of ending at a ferrule or adapter as on some bait-casting rods and on some boat and offshore rods, which use detachable butts.

Considering the low cost of any butt cap, the simplest solution for any cracking, breaking, and so on is to replace it. If a similar type of butt cap is not available through a tackle shop or specialty supply business, then a rubber crutch tip will also work. Crutch tips are available in two lengths and four or five sizes. Similar to these are the firm plastic slip-over chair tips that also come in sizes suitable for fishing rods. The main disadvantage is that these are slippery, which makes it more difficult to prevent sliding and damage when propping a rod against a gunwale or on a hardwood floor. Their hard material makes gluing more difficult, too.

When replacing butt caps, first remove the old cap (you can take it along when you buy a new one, or get its measurements). If the cap is loose, it should easily slide off. If it is damaged but not loose, you should be able to cut it off carefully with a sharp knife or chisel.

Once the old cap is off, you are ready to put on the new one. First file or rasp any old glue off the end of the rod. Then use a rasp or small roll of sandpaper to rough up the inside of the butt cap for a better grip by the glue. Use a 24-hour epoxy glue or rod-finish epoxy, and slide the butt cap on tightly. The epoxy rod finish (such as Flex Coat) is excellent because it is flexible, as are the flexible butt caps.

Some glue will probably ooze from the junction of the butt cap with the rod handle, and it should be wiped up immediately. If the rod has a foam handle, wrap the end of the rod handle with several layers of masking tape, wrap the butt cap the same way, slide the parts together, wipe up any glue, then remove the tape to uncover a clean surface. Once the butt cap is in place, place the rod upright with the butt on the floor to prevent the butt cap from loosening or sliding off.

If your rod has a swaged aluminum butt cap, and it is only damaged but not loose, you may have to heat the cap to loosen the glue. Wrap the handle up to the butt cap with a damp rag to protect the grip and use repeated quick passes with a propane torch until the butt cap loosens. Use another rag or heavy gloves to avoid burning yourself, and remove the butt cap. If you don't care about the butt cap, gently applied pliers will also work. If the butt cap is an aluminum sleeve with a rubber end and will not come off, use a knife to cut away the rubber end and then use the propane torch to remove the aluminum.

You can also use a cutting tool to remove a metal or aluminum butt cap. These include a grinder, a small cut-off wheel as a grinder, or hand tool such as the Dremel Moto-Tool. With these, it is possible to grind or cut through the butt cap at several points, then pry it loose with a chisel or screwdriver. When doing this, be sure to wrap the handle with heavy layers of masking tape to prevent damage to the grip.

With a damaged grip or splintered wood handle on a boat rod, you may wish to save the aluminum butt cap or aluminum gimbel knock (a slotted butt cap for use on boat rods, which fits the rod into a holder or belt for fighting fish) for a new handle. Use care in applying heat and use only a rag or heavy gloves to remove the butt cap. Clean it up and reapply as outlined above.

Flexible butt caps are best glued in place with an epoxy rod finish, since the rod finish will stay more flexible than most glues. For this step, wrap both parts (butt cap and end of rod grip) with masking tape to make cleanup easier.

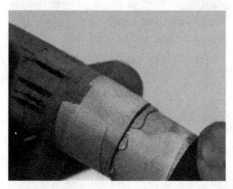

Fitting the butt cap in place. Note that the glue that oozes out can be easily cleaned up, and the tape removed, leaving the parts completely clean.

Some lightweight spinning rods have a small aluminum plate that serves as a butt cap. These will have a small metal extension that goes into the rod blank and helps to glue the plate in place. The best way to remove this is to slide a thin-bladed knife or razor blade around the edge to loosen the plate.

Grips

Grips or handles are made of many materials. Cork, foam (Hypalon, Foamlite, and other synthetics); wood, often varnished as on boat rod handles; and aluminum, used on offshore rods, such as the UniButt system on trolling game rods, are all used.

Aluminum Handles These can't really be repaired, unless repair means replacing a part, such as a sliding hood, knurled ring, ferrule collet nut, or something similar that can be easily slipped off and replaced.

Wood Handles These are on the rear of many saltwater boat rods. They are seldom severely damaged, but do suffer severe wear. If the damage is severe, such as a bad crack, it is best to replace the wood handle. Remove the reel seat and butt cap and replace the wood part. Some wood handles separate from the rest of the rod and attach with a ferrule or adapter that fits into the forward end of the reel seat and usually is held down with a collet nut. These are easy to replace, because they require only removal of the reel seat and knock, then regluing these on a new handle.

Use the methods listed above to remove the butt cap (often an aluminum or chrome-plated brass gimbel knock) and the reel seat. These are usually metal (few plastic or graphite-fill reel seats are available), so the best removal is with a propane torch, heating slowly and evenly to melt and break down the glue so that the reel seat and knock can be removed. Do *not* use a torch or heat on anything other than metal reel seats and gimbels. Be sure to use only heavy gloves or a damp rag to grasp these parts, because pliers will mar the finish. Once removed, clean out the reel seat and knock and use 24-hour epoxy glue to remount them on a new wood handle.

Some saltwater rods with wood handles are built on long, straight-through blanks, with the wood handle drilled and glued to the blank. Heat won't work here. Instead, place the handle in a vise and use only firm pressure so the handle and the blank it contains will not be crushed. Then use a chisel to carefully plane away the wood until you reach the blank. Repeat this on several sides until the blank is exposed or you can pry off the remaining wood. An alternative method is to use a carpenter's plane to remove the wood. Clamp the handle horizontally in a vise so that the side of the handle is above the surface of the vise. This will prevent the vise from nicking the plane blade.

In most cases, wood handles are designed for specific brands and sizes of reel seats, making regluing easy. If this is not the case, you may have to build up the recess for the reel seat, if the reel seat is loose on the handle, or thin the recess, if the wood is too thick for the existing reel seat. The best way to build up a seat is to use heavy thread or light cord as a shim to fill the gap. Don't use a circular wrap, which may be pushed out of position as the reel seat is slid on, but run strands of thread over the end of the handle and down the other side to make cord strips that are parallel with the reel seat.

Depending on how much shim you need, you can have four, six, eight, or more spines of cord along the reel seat recess. Keep the cord or thread in place with masking tape or wraps at the middle of the handle. The shims will keep the reel seat parallel to the handle, and the cord cannot be pushed out of position as you glue the reel seat on the handle. Once close to the final position, cut the cord, then push the reel seat down the last $\frac{1}{2}$ inch so that no cord will show. The same method will work for positioning gimbel knocks, although too much space here will leave a gap between the handle and the gimbel. If this occurs, it might be better to cut the end of the handle back $\frac{1}{4}$ inch at a time until you get a proper fit. This only works on handles that taper to a thinner diameter at the gimbel knock.

The best way to cut down a handle to fit a reel seat or gimbel knock is to decrease the size on a lathe, using inside/outside calipers to check for the proper diameter, or removing the handle to fit the reel seat and/or knock. Lacking a lathe, use a wood rasp, working with equal strokes every 90° around the reel seat recess so that you remove equal amounts of wood on all sides. Once close to the right size, remove the corners to make the cross section into a rough octagon, then round off the wood with a rasp to bring it to the final size. A fine finish is not required, because it will be glued into the reel seat.

If working with a rod requiring a straight-through handle, you will have to get a drilled-through handle, then add the reel seat and gimbel knock as described. Use a straightened coat hanger to run 24-hour epoxy glue into the hole, smear some on the lower part of the blank, and insert the blank slowly into the handle. To prevent glue from getting on the blank or reel seat, wrap both these parts (at the point where they will fit) with several layers of masking tape. Once in place, wipe up any glue and remove the masking tape.

Wood handles with peeling, worn, or damaged finishes can be easily refinished. Wrap layers of masking tape around the reel seat and gimbel knock or butt cap. This will protect their metal finishes as you remove the handle finish. To remove the old finish, use a paint-and-finish stripper and follow the directions on the can, or sand the handle down to bare wood. When the wood is clean and bare, add a new finish of waterproof urethane, epoxy, spray epoxy, or spar varnish. Unless using a thick epoxy, add several coats for maximum protection.

Cork Grips These are subject to gouges, chipping, and even blows that can ruin several of the rings that are used to make up grips like this. Several repair possibilities are possible, depending upon the extent of the damage. For slight chips and gouges, clean and refill the mar.

To do this, clean out any loose or cracked areas in the gouge. Do not sand it smooth or try to make it completely concave or dishlike. This will make it harder for the glue to grip the cork and increase the likelihood of the repair falling out.

Once the gouged area is clean and prepared, use a rasp to make some cork filings, preferably from high-quality cork. Wine corks, bass bug bodies, or cork craft

Small dents and dings in cork handles can be repaired with a mixture of cork dust and glue. Force the glue/cork mixture into any holes or gouges. Allow to cure overnight and file and sand to shape.

items will work for this. Remove any large chunks so that only cork "sawdust" is left. Mix this with a thick glue. I like to use waterproof or water-repellent carpenter's glue such as Elmer's Aliphatic Carpenter's Glue, which is thick, cork colored, water resistant, and easy to work with. Epoxy glues are also good, if you carefully limit the amount you use. Epoxy glues are harder and more difficult to work if you do not get the right cork-to-glue mix.

Mix the glue thoroughly with the cork, using only enough glue to hold the cork together. Spread glue on the gouge, force in the cork mix, and build it up into a slight mound above the grip. When cured completely, use a rasp to rough the repaired area down toward the grip. Use successively finer grades of sandpaper to finish this, smoothing the cork until it matches the surface and shape of the grip. At this point, you may wish to protectively tape the butt cap, reel seat, rod, or any other parts and use the finest sandpaper to smooth and clean the rest of the cork grip to match the lighter color of the repair area.

Deeper gouges, those that remove a section of the grip, can be repaired in one of two similar ways. First, if the damaged portion is only on one side of the grip, you can remove it and replace that section of cork with cork ring pieces that can be sanded to shape, finish, and size. Missing cork rings, or damage all around a grip section, can be repaired by removing the rings in that area and replacing them with new ones. In both cases you will need some cork rod-building rings. These are available in ½-inch thickness, various hole sizes, and $1\frac{1}{8}$-, $1\frac{1}{4}$-, $1\frac{1}{2}$-, and 2-inch outer diameters. The hole size does not much matter, but if you have a choice get the smallest hole available. Holes can be enlarged easier than they can be filled up. Such rings may be available at your local tackle shop or through mail-order rod-building supply houses.

When damage is on one side of the grip, use a rasp to file down the area, taking out a section that will not cut into the rod blank, but will be squared off. The section must be in ½-inch length increments. This is necessary because the cork rings you will use for repair are all ½ inch thick. Next, cut the cork ring in half through the hole. Use a rasp to lightly roughen the cut surface. Check to make sure that the cork rings fit snugly into the space provided and make any adjust-

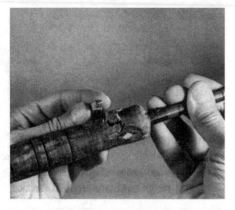

Damaged corks in cork handles can be repaired without removing and replacing the entire handle. Damage to several rings in the cork handle is shown here.

The damaged portion must be removed in increments of $\frac{1}{2}$ inch. Here, the cork is being removed with a file. Take care not to damage the rod blank.

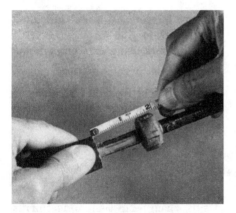

Opening gap is measured to be sure that it is in increments of $\frac{1}{2}$ inch, so that the cork rings will fit properly.

Replacement cork rings are cut in half as shown to be fitted into place.

ments necessary. The cork rings will be thicker than the grip but will be sanded down after the glue cures.

Spread carpenter's or epoxy glue onto the grip's damaged area, on the cut, and on the facing surfaces of each cork ring. Put each cork ring in place. Wipe up any excess glue, especially if using epoxy because epoxy is more difficult to work with, sand to shape and size when cured. Use rubber bands or masking tape to secure the cork rings in place as the glue cures. If using rubber bands, place a cushion of cardboard on the side of the grip opposite the repair, to prevent the rubber bands from cutting into the grip. Once cured, remove the tape or bands, and use a rasp, file, and fine sandpaper to shape and finish the cork repair.

Repairing more extensive damage is done similarly, except that an entire section of cork grip must be removed and replaced. To do this, use a rasp to remove

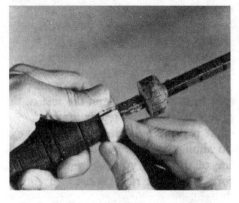

Replacement cork ring halves being fitted into place.

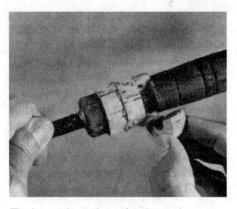

The last cork ring being fitted into place.

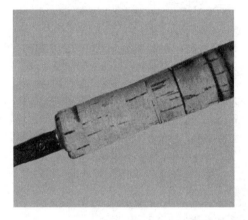

After filing and sanding, the replacement cork rings fit perfectly into the old grip.

the old damaged cork. The section removed must again be in ½-inch increments. Use cork rings that are larger than the diameter of the handle so that they can be sanded to fit. In most cases, 1⅛-inch-diameter rings are fine for fly grips, 1¼-inch are fine for spinning- and popping-rod grips, and 1½-inch are fine for saltwater and surf-rod grips.

When the rod blank is exposed, make sure that the facing corks in the remaining grip are parallel and squared off. Cut the replacement rings in half and at a slight angle for maximum gluing surface. Be sure to keep each of the two halves together or keyed in some way.

Spread glue on all the adjoining surfaces—the rings, rod blank, half holes in the cork, cut portions of the cork rings, facing corks in the grip. Add half rings on one side because this will wedge them into place. Add the other half rings, making sure that they join with their mate to prevent mismatching. Then rotate the rings so that no joint is in line with another. This will create a stronger bond. Wrap with tape or rubber bands and allow to cure overnight. After curing, remove any tape or bands and rasp, file, and sand to shape. This method allows cork rings to be added to any fore or rear grip, without having to remove the remainder of the grip or removing guides to rebuild the handle from scratch.

New handles for rods can be made from cork rings. These cork rings are reamed out to fit on a rod blank.

Cork rings are glued in place using a waterproof glue and gluing to both the back and also the cork-to-cork surfaces. Guides must be removed from the blank or from the butt section of the rod to slide the cork rings in place.

To complete the handle, the cork is filed first on four sides, then eight. After this step, it is easy to round off the edges and smooth the cork for a handle.

Shaping the rod handle with a rasp.

Finished cork handle. This will be removed from the dowel and then glued onto a rod.

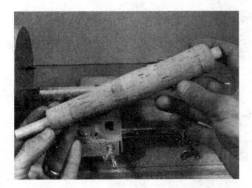

Hypalon or Synthetic Grips These can't really be repaired as can cork, but they can be replaced on rear grips. With a damaged rear grip, remove the butt cap and cut off the old grip. Often the best way to do this is to use a sharp razor blade to cut down the full length of the grip to the rod blank, peeling the grip off as you do the shell from a steamed shrimp.

Once the old grip is off, you can add a new one from the rear, instead of from the tip end as the rod was built. This does present difficulties, because all grips like this are best made using a grip with a smaller-diameter hole than that of the blank to assure a tight fit. In building rods, this is no problem because of the taper; grips are seated from the tip end of all blanks. During this repair job, you must get a new grip up over the thicker butt end. There are several ways to do this. One is to use a grip with a diameter close to that of the blank, and use epoxy glue to hold the grip in place without slipping. The second is to make a double-tapered dowel (one taper to roughly fit the blank, the other end to lead the grip on) so that the grip will slide on.

You must use a lubricant to slide the grip in place. Glue usually is best used for this. Spread it inside the hole of the grip and on the dowel and blank. Wrap several protective layers of masking tape around the end of the reel seat and the end of the grip. Push the grip in place. Often a good way to do this is to use a board with a center hole just larger than the blank diameter. Place this board into a vise. Then, using a dowel as long as the grip, place the dowel into this hole and push the rod to move the grip up on the blank. Do not push too hard, because the blank might split. Once the grip is in place, remove the dowel, "milk" the grip into the shape that you wish, and wipe up any glue that has oozed between the grip and reel seat. Remove the tape, glue the butt cap back on (use tape to prevent glue stains on the cap or grip), and allow to cure overnight.

There is no way to replace synthetic foregrips other than removing any guides that might be on the butt section. If the rod does not have any guides on this section, such as on some popping off-center ferruled rods or short-section pack rods, then the grip can be cut off and the new grip can be slid down the blank to a previously glue-coated section.

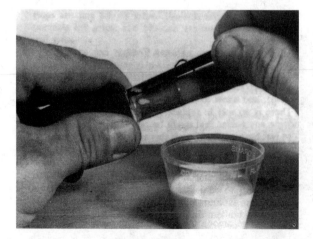

Sometimes foam handles and grips can become loose. There is no easy solution to this short of a difficult replacement, but one possible solution is to open up the gap between the rod blank and the foam and force glue into this opening. Water-based glue is best, since cleanup will be easier.

Reel Seats

Reel seats are among the most difficult parts to repair. If the reel seat is completely damaged and unusable, then it can only be replaced. Take off the grip, heat the reel seat to remove it if metal or saw it off if it's graphite or plastic, replace with a new reel seat, and remount the grip following the above directions.

A new reel seat may or may not be the same diameter as the one removed. If it has a smaller inside diameter, you may have to remove some or all of the bushing material from the rod blank. If you remove it all, you will have to build up a new one. This is done by lightly coating the rod blank with epoxy glue, and wrapping cord tightly and repeatedly around the blank to build the cord up to the correct diameter. With each layer or two of the cord, add more glue. This should be a spiraling wrap that will leave open areas. Finish the cord by tying off with several half hitches. Add more epoxy glue, wrap the ends of the reel seat and the butting grip with tape to ease cleaning, and slide the reel seat in place.

Do the same thing to build up an existing bushing. In these cases, though, one or two layers of cord are often enough. Avoid using too large a reel seat, because it will not match the ends of the grips.

It is also possible to build up or add to bushings with adhesive paper tape or masking tape. Be particularly careful with masking tape because it is flexible and spongy and will break down in time. When using tape as a bushing ring, be sure to use enough glue to bond the reel seat directly to the rod blank. This is done by making several shims of tape rings at each end of the reel seat area, partly sliding the reel seat on, pouring glue into the open reel seat, sliding it on the rest of the way, then placing the rod vertical so that the glue will cure around the rod blank and out to the reel seat.

A vexing problem with a reel seat is when it works but is loose. There are, unfortunately, no simple solutions. You can remove the grip and reel seat, replace the reel seat (and bushing if needed—poorly glued or tape-type bushings are a principal cause of loose reel seats). Lacking this somewhat complex repair, other solutions include drilling several or more holes in the reel seat and bushing area and using a small syringe to inject epoxy glue into the area that's slipping.

Types of bushings that can be used for replacing reel seats. Left to right: fiber bushing, cork bushing, wrapped paper tape bushing, wrapped cord bushing, masking tape bushing, cord axis bushing, and thread axis bushing.

You can also use a hacksaw to cut out the center barrel portion, remove its bushing, slide the ends (fixed hood and threaded barrel/sliding hood) to the center, reglue them in their original positions, then build up a cork insert section in the reel seat using the half cork rings as previously described. This gives a custom, professional result, although it does take work. Make sure that both hoods are lined up with the guides when gluing them in place.

Guides

Guides can seldom be repaired, but they can be easily replaced. Guide repairs include only the following:

1. Frame repairs: Bent, not broken, frames can be returned to the original shape with flat-nose pliers. Work slowly and carefully to avoid breaking any bends.
2. Grooved wire-ring guides: Slight grooves in wire-ring guides can be temporarily repaired by using crocus or fine emery cloth to polish out the grooving and restore the ring's smooth surface. This is only a temporary solution, however; ultimately the guides will have to be replaced. Grooving in metal rings is caused by the line running in one place and wearing through the guide. Even after polishing, friction in this spot will continue. Polishing is only a stopgap measure.
3. Roller guides: Guides such as those by AFTCO can be repaired by replacing the parts of the guide. These parts include the roller, pin, bushing, and screw of the guide. These can be replaced without affecting the frame or guide wrap.

Guide replacement is easy, because it requires only cutting through the old thread to remove the guide, wrapping a new guide in place, and covering the thread with a rod-wrap finish.

Use a sharp razor blade to cut off the old wrap. Use the blade as if it was a carpenter's plane to shave through the full length of the thread wrap. If you cut straight down, you can go through the gel-coat finish of the rod and into the fibers that make up the rod. Shaving allows you to take off successive layers of threading

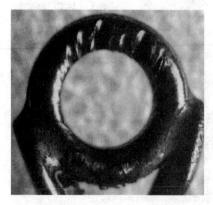

Grooved tiptops like this require immediate replacement to prevent line damage and lost fish.

In replacing guides, old wraps must be cut off. The best way to do this is to use a razor blade like a small carpenter's plane, slicing through the wrap but not the blank.

until the blank is barely exposed. Then, if color preserver was used on the wrap, just peel the wrap off.

If color preserver was not used, the epoxy penetrates the wrap so you must continue shaving the finish and wrap, taking care not to damage the rod blank. After removal, you might find a few threads at each end fastened to the rod, but these are easily removed. You will be replacing the guide in the same spot, so lightly sand any remaining finish at the ends of the wrap with a manicure emery board. Take care not to cut into the blank, or to scar the finish of the bare rod.

Use the same ring size and style for replacement as the guide removed. With companies rapidly changing in the component parts field, you may not get an exact match, but should be able to come close. Guides close in style are important, however. An ultralight rod refitted with a double-foot guide might feel sluggish or slow. The same could happen when changing a five-guide rod to six guides, or using a large-sized guide ring. If you suspect this problem may develop, tape the guides on and cast or fish with the rod briefly to see if the guide harms the rod's action or power.

Once a guide is selected, file the end of the guide to a knifelike edge. This is necessary for a smooth and even transition of the thread from the blank to the guide foot; otherwise there will be a gap in the thread at the end of the guide foot. Also, lightly rub the bottom of the guide foot to remove any burrs that might have resulted from filing both feet.

Thread comes in different sizes and colors. Be sure to use only rod-wrapping thread, which is a special nylon, because other threads (cotton or synthetics for sewing) lack the necessary strength and sleekness, resulting in a poor wrap. Use size A thread for fly rods, ultralight spinning rods, light spincast rods, and light casting rods. Use size D for heavy saltwater fly rods, medium-action casting rods, medium to heavy spinning rods, and most freshwater and light saltwater tackle, such as light boat rods, surf rods, and boat spinning rods. Use E thread for heavy surf rods, 50- to 80-pound-test class trolling rods, heavy jigging and boat rods, and similar tackle. EE thread is made for the heaviest rods such as offshore shark rods and International Game Fish Association 130-pound-class or heavier trolling tackle.

Pick the same thread color as that used by the rod maker. This may be difficult

SELECTING THE PROPER PERFECTION GUIDES AND TOP

Choosing the correct size guide

Determine the Perfection guide size for your rod building requirement by referring to the chart below. When sizing a guide needing replacement, simply use the chart to match its outside ring diameter to the corresponding Perfection size.

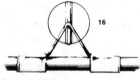

Lay your rod on this page as shown. Look straight down on the guide ring from above and match it with the Perfection guide closest in size

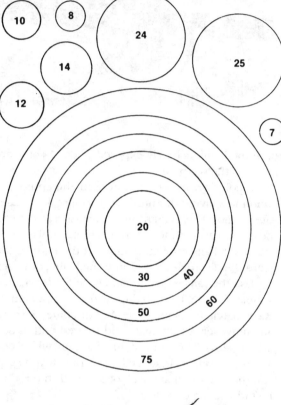

Choosing the right top

Top sizes are diameters measured in $^{1}/_{64}$ inches.

This handy dot-chart will help you determine which size top is right for your rod. Measure down the rod shaft ½" from the tip and mark that spot on the rod. Place the rod on this page and move it from dot to dot until you find the dot that most closely matches the rod's diameter at the spot you marked—That's the approximate rod top tube size you need.

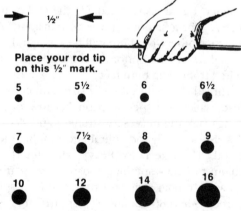

Place your rod tip on this ½" mark.

5	5½	6	6½
7	7½	8	9
10	12	14	16

Tiptop and guide gauge for choosing the correct size of guide. *Courtesy of Perfection Tip.*

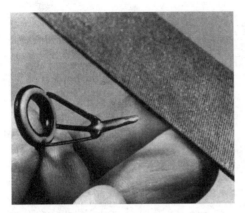

All guide feet of all guides must be filed to a knife edge before being wrapped in place. This prevents gaps in the wrapping.

on factory rods because some manufacturers use colors that are not available commercially, so pick the closest color possible. It is often best to choose a slightly lighter color, and then use no color preserver, which will cause the thread color to darken when epoxy is applied. (Lighter thread colors will get lighter if no preserver is used.)

If you are concerned about the match, do a test wrap on a scrap piece of rod or dowel to check the final color after coating with a finish. One important point here is that the lack of color preserver will also make the thread slightly transparent. A guide with a bright frame might be visible through the thread wrap, and a black guide with a filed (bright) end foot might also show through.

When you have assembled all your materials, file and tape the guide in place with masking tape. Suitably thin ⅛- inch masking tape is available from some rod supply houses or from auto shops that specialize in body work (the tape is used for pin-striping). Otherwise, take regular masking tape and cut thin strips, each several inches long. Tape the guide so that the foot's end is exposed so that you can begin wrapping the thread on the guide before removing the tape. Tape the guide in place, centering it so that there will be equal-length wraps on each guide foot and so that the guide is lined up with the tiptop, and reel hoods.

Rod builders have special tools for wrapping rods and maintaining thread tension. If you have these, great, if not, you can easily get by with a teacup, telephone book, and two sheets of typing paper. Place the thread in the teacup (to keep it from rolling off the table or around the floor), run the thread through the two sheets of unused typing paper (to keep the thread clean) in the center of the phone book. The weight of the phone book creates the thread tension, which can be adjusted by the thread's position in the pages. For more tension, just add books on top. Hold the rod in your hands or put the rod on a cardboard box that has the front removed and notches cut in the front top sides to create Vs to support the rod.

Roger Seiders of Flex Coat likes a different method. He places the cup holding the thread behind a chair, runs the thread over the chair seat, and sits on the chair to maintain tension. He rolls the rod on his lap away from him and so he can watch the wraps as they are laid down.

Begin the wrap in the same spot as the original wrap, making several turns

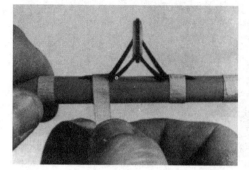

Begin a wrap on a rod by taping the guides down and also taping the borders of the wraps. Note that the guides wrapped down leave the end of the guide foot exposed so that the thread wrap can be begun before the tape is removed.

around the blank and over the thread to secure the thread end. Make sure the threads are parallel and have no gaps between them. After six to eight turns, cut off excess thread from the end. Continue wrapping, rotating the rod and maintaining thread tension. Watch for gaps or overlapping of threads. The best way to do this is to keep the thread at a slight angle to the previous wrap so that each wrap is laid down tightly against the previous one. Use care at the beginning of the guide foot, and wrap up on the guide foot.

Remove the tape, continue wrapping until you are six to eight turns from the edge of the guide frame. At this point, wrap down a doubled loop of thread with the loop end pointing toward the center of the guide. Continue wrapping to the guide frame. Holding the thread, cut it, and insert the end through the loop. Pull the loop through the wraps, at the same time pulling the end of the thread to secure it. Cut the excess thread, using a razor blade to cut straight down between the wraps and cut the end. Use your thumbnail or a smooth pen as a burnisher to close up this gap and any other spaces that might have developed during the wrapping.

Turn the rod around and repeat this on the other guide foot. This type of

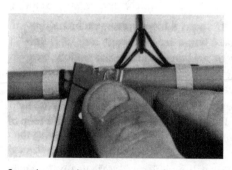

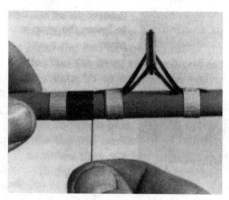

Start the wrap by wrapping over the thread about four to six turns and then cutting any excess thread as shown.

Continuing the wrap.

The wrap as it begins to go up over the end of the guide foot.

wrap is similar to other rod wraps that might have to be replaced, such as the simple decorative wrap about the handle, wraps at the ferrules, and the short wrap at the tiptop.

Heavy rods may have a wrap underneath the guide wrap and this should also be replaced. Remove all wraps, make the underwrap on the rod, then add the guides as outlined. Underwraps are aesthetically pleasing and provide a good cushion between the rod blank and the metal guide foot on big-game rods.

After the wraps are completed, they must be protected with a finish. To prevent the thread color from changing, you must use a color preserver. Color preservers come in two bases: solvent and acrylic. Solvents are usually clear and have a distinct lacquer smell. The acrylics have a different smell and often look white and milky. Both preservers should cover the wrap, soaking it, with any excess blotted up. Use a small disposable brush to apply the color preserver, beginning with the wraps at the tip end and working down to the butt end of the rod. Then return to the tip end to blot any residue with a paper towel or napkin. A second layer can be added within minutes after the first coat, but then wait 24 to 36 hours before adding the rod fin-

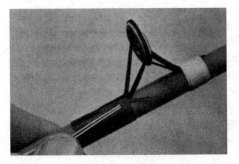

Finish the wrap by wrapping over a loop of thread and tucking the end of the wrap through the loop. Here the loop is being pulled through to fasten the wrap in place.

Continue to pull the thread through with the loop of extra thread.

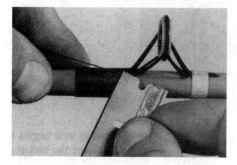

Finished wrap, burnished to smooth the wraps in place.

Once the thread is pulled through, cut the end with a razor blade, as shown. Another way of doing this is to open up a gap in the wrap, and cut straight down with the razor blade.

Finished wraps must be protected with a coat of color preserver. For best results, apply liberally and then blot any excess.

ish. A good way to check if enough time has elapsed is to closely smell the wrap. If you still smell the color preserver, wait until you can't. It is also important to use the right preserver. For example, Flex Coat recommends only their color preserver because other lacquer-base color preservers might cause the epoxy finish to color in time. Following color preserver, rod finish (epoxy or other type) must be added to protect the wrap. The color preserver will *not* protect the wrap — only preserve the thread color. See instructions in chapter 2.

Tiptops These guides differ from others on the rod because they are attached by a tube that fits on the end of the rod blank, instead of a frame connected to one or two feet that are wrapped in place on the rod. Tiptops can become loose and require retightening. If a tiptop is loose, the easy solution is to slide it gently off the rod. Use a toothpick or paper clip to clean old glue out of the tube and with a pocketknife or razor blade, scrape any glue off the end of the rod blank. When scraping glue off the blank, take care not to damage the thread wrap. The wrap

Cementing new tiptop on rod. Use of heat-set cement is most popular as shown here, but regular glues can be used.

here is strictly decorative and does not hold the tiptop in place so it does not have to be removed to reglue or replace the tiptop.

When the old glue is removed from the tube and the blank, thoroughly mix the epoxy, insert some into the tube with a paper clip, smear a little on the rod blank, and slide the tiptop back in place. Use clean rags or paper towels to wipe any cement that flows out of the tube onto the thread wrap. Also carefully check the end of the tiptop, because some tiptops have a small hole in the end of the tube through which glue can flow. If this occurs, wipe the glue away with a toothpick and clean up this area.

Glue is very runny right after being mixed, so you may find it difficult to adjust the rod so that the tiptop is precisely aligned with the rod guides. One method is to lay the rod flat between two supports so that the guides hang straight down. Then the tiptop can be adjusted so it also hangs down by the weight of the guide ring, and automatically lines up. It also helps to make a last-minute alignment check as the glue begins to set. For 5-minute epoxy, check this after 2 to 3 minutes; with standard epoxy, wait about 30 minutes, then make any adjustments when the tiptop is still movable but before the glue completely sets.

Rod Finish

Older rods will sometimes experience peeling or flaking of the factory finish. It might seem simple to refinish the rod, but the longevity of the results often leaves something to be desired. Brush-on and spray epoxies or urethane finishes can be applied to the rod. The result will be beautiful for several years or so, but it will not be nearly as durable as the higher-quality, factory finish.

In cases of severe peeling or wear, though, a new finish might be the only solution. Other cases where refinishing is required include rods that are rebuilt with the guides repositioned. (Guides may be repositioned because a broken tip required rebuilding, the rod's function changed, or the number of the guides or the length of the grip/handle was changed.) In these cases, refinishing is almost a must, because the original position of the wraps will show ridges where the thread has grooved the surface of the blank.

As a result of color changes and sun on the exposed blank, you can never hope to refinish a rod so that the previous guide positions do not show.

To refinish a rod you can remove the guides and refinish the blank, then rewrap the guides, or you can refinish the rod with the guides still in place. If the guides are damaged, threads are frayed, and so on, pick the first choice; if the guides and wraps are fine, pick the latter.

To refinish a rod in either case, you cannot allow the rod to ride on a central support as you do when finishing wraps, because this would mar the new finish. Several solutions are possible. If the guides are on the rod, run a thin dowel or old rod blank through the tiptop and first two to three guides, then rest the dowel on a support to hold the rod as a motor turns the butt end. If finishing a stout rod blank, with the tiptop removed, you can run a dowel or rod blank into the hollow end of the blank and rest this extension on the support. For completed rods, you can also tie a loop of cord to the tiptop, attach a ball-bearing swivel, tie in another loop, and fasten this loop to a support just beyond the end of the tiptop. This way, the rod can be turned to cure the finish and the swivel will prevent tangles.

Finishes can be brushed on, as outlined for wrapping guides, or sprayed on with long, even strokes. In most cases, the thinner coat of spray finishes does not require turning the rod. You should check the spray coating carefully as you work and immediately thereafter to ensure that it is even.

Broken Rods

Repairing a broken rod is not difficult in most cases, but it is time consuming and requires the right materials, such as a scrap blank that can be used for reinforcing the broken area.

Rod tips will frequently break just a few inches down from the end. The best repair is not to try to reinforce and replace the broken section, but to remove the broken section and add a new tiptop to the broken end. If the break is a split, splintered break, or break where the fiber peels off, this may not be possible. Fortunately, this is seldom the case. If the rod is splintered, you may not be able to repair it. If the splintering is slight, you can cut the rod blank back to a point below the splintered fibers and adjust (rewrap) the position of the remaining guides as desired.

With surf, some spinning, steelhead, offshore, boat, and similarly large rods that have guides far apart, you can usually sand down a clean break and remount a tiptop, using a larger size to fit the new, larger diameter of the rod tip.

For casting or fly rods, in which the guides are close together, the best solution is often to remove the top guide, cut the rod back to this point, and replace the guide with a new tiptop. A new tiptop is necessary because the taper of the rod blank will be too wide for the original tiptop. Use a fine-blade hacksaw (32 teeth per inch) or fine triangular file to score the rod blank where you want to cut it. When the outer skin is scored, file or saw through the blank slowly and evenly. Replace the tiptop and wraps following the previous directions.

For breaks farther down on the rod, repairs are often possible but *only* if the break is a clean one and not splintered or damaged over a large area. If a one-piece rod breaks at, or below, its halfway point, consider adding a ferrule. Pick a ferrule

Split-bamboo rods can sometimes be repaired. *If the damage is to a fine bamboo rod, first check with a reliable repairman or rod appraiser for value of the rod. Home repairs like this are best only with inexpensive bamboo rods of little value.* In this splintered damage, toothpicks are used to hold apart the strips of the rod for gluing. The cord is used for wrapping the rod while the glue cures.

After the glue is applied, wrap the rod firmly with cord. This cord serves to clamp the parts together and will be removed once the glue is cured.

that will snugly fit on the rod or, if mail-ordering a ferrule, measure the rod carefully about 1 inch below the break.

Cut or file both ends of the break smooth, then roughen them with fine sandpaper or emery cloth. Check the ferrules for a good fit. If the fit is too tight, you may have to sand the rod blank slightly. If it is too loose, shim the rod blank with thread, bringing the thread up over the ends of the break and down the sides of the rod blank so that the shim threads are parallel to the blank. Coat the blank with good waterproof epoxy glue, smear some on the inside of each ferrule part, and slide the ferrules in place. Wipe away excess glue, cut any threads if required (if thread was used for a shim), and allow to cure overnight before testing and using.

To repair a break without adding a new ferrule the break must be clean, and you need to closely match the broken ends. You also need a scrap piece of fiberglass or graphite the same size and roughly the same taper as the broken rod. Remove the butt cap of the rod, cut a section of the scrap blank to fit the break area, slide and glue it into place, and glue the broken tip end onto this splice. Follow with a long wrap of fine thread to reinforce the rod and give it hoop strength in this area.

This will not work if this is a powerful graphite rod and broken in the tip end, because the thin-spliced section probably will not be strong enough to hold up under the stresses on the rod. There is no simple rule for the diameter or action limiting this type of repair, but the more powerful the rod and the less inside diameter you have to work with, the greater the danger of later rod breakage.

The basic steps for this operation once you have the proper materials are as follows:

1. Remove the butt cap of the rod if the break is in the butt section or if the rod is one piece.
2. Slide the scrap piece of blank into the rod at the broken end to determine the junction of the fit. Mark this spot on the scrap rod.
3. Cut the scrap rod 3 inches above and below this mark. Extend the cut shim (splicing) section into the rod, using a second blank section or straightened coat hanger to slide the blank in place. Pull the shim snug and then wiggle it slightly sideways to determine the degree of play or looseness in the blank. If it's loose, determine which end of the shim blank is loose, remove the shim, and sand the required area.
4. Replace the shim and check for proper fit. Repeat until the shim fits.
5. Repeat the above with the shim in place, checking for a proper fit of the broken tip end over the shim.
6. Coat the thicker half of the splicing-blank section with epoxy glue and slide it in place. Once it extends from the end of the blank, pull it into place and remove excess glue from the blank. Coat the protruding end of the shim with glue. Carefully slide the tip section onto the shim, making sure that the shim does not loosen. (You may wish to wait until the glue cures in the butt before replacing the tip section. This prevents pushing the splice or shim back down into the rod.)

    Once in place, match up the sections, and remove any excess glue. If there is a gap between the two broken sections (as will occur in a slight crushing break), allow some glue to remain in the gap to fill the space to the level of the blanks for wrapping. Allow to cure overnight.
7. Use thread the color of the blank to wrap the break. Begin 2 inches below the break and wrap 2 inches above it. Coat with epoxy finish as you would with a guide wrap.

Some tips for working with stout rods include using scrap pieces of graphite or glass blank to build up a shim section of two or three layers for added strength. The best way to check to see if this is needed is to flex the rod near the break and compare the strength and flex with the scrap blank/shim material. To do this, make up layers by gluing smaller sections into larger ones until you add enough wall thickness to the shim to be used in the repair.

Ferrules, Collets, and Butt Adapters

Metal ferrules are rarely used on modern rods, but you can still find them on older models. A method of restoring bent ferrules was mentioned in chapter 2. The only real repair for metal ferrules, however, is replacement. The difficulty is finding parts, because the major manufacturers of these ferrules are out of business. Good ferrules—read expensive—of nickel silver are still available for custom, usually bamboo, fly-rod construction and repairs.

To replace a metal ferrule, first remove the old ferrule. If it is already loose, gently pull it off. If it is not loose, protect the rod with several layers of masking tape, then use a cigarette lighter or alcohol lamp to heat the metal while turning the rod to distribute the heat evenly. Pull the heated and loosened ferrule straight off the rod with pliers. Most repairs require new male and female pieces, so also do this with the other ferrule.

Clean the blank to remove old glue and, if necessary, rough the blank lightly with steel wool to give the blank some "tooth" for a better gluing bond. Test the new ferrule set on the blank for fit. If the fit is too tight, sand the blank to reduce its diameter. Do this with care, because sanding reduces the strength of the blank in that area. Thin-walled blanks allow almost no sanding.

You can fix a fit that is too loose by cutting back the butt section of the blank slightly, in $\frac{1}{4}$-inch increments. This will allow fitting on a slightly thicker area of the blank because of its taper. You can't cut back the other side, because the increasing taper of the tip will make any fit looser. The disadvantage of cutting the rod is that if too much is removed, the rod's two sections will be slightly uneven.

A better method is to use shims of rod-wrapping thread as spacers between the blank and the ferrule. The secret is to run the shims of thread parallel to the axis of the rod. To do this, use masking tape to secure a thread several inches from the rod end. Run the thread parallel to the blank and up over the end, down the other side; secure with masking tape. Do this several times evenly around the blank, to build up two, four, six, or eight shims. How many depends on the blank diameter and the amount of shimming needed. Shim thickness can also be controlled by the size of the thread. Use A thread for light shimming, D for heavier shimming, and E for extra-heavy shimming. The advantage of parallel thread and shim placement over circular thread wrap is that the latter can be pushed out of place when the ferrule is mounted, whereas the parallel shims will retain their original position.

Once the shims are taped in place, mark the rod for the final position of the end of the ferrule. Be careful when measuring open-end female ferrules, because there is no separation between the part glued to the rod and the part fitting the male ferrule. When measuring the male ferrule, add $\frac{1}{8}$ inch for glue and shim spacing.

Once the rod is marked, spread glue inside the ferrule and over the rod. For

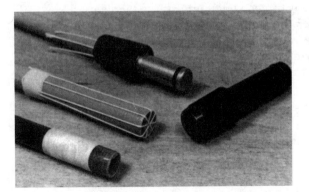

Shims for seating replacement ferrules and butt adapters on rods are easily made from cord, by wrapping around the blank (foreground) or stringing the cord along the axis of the blank (middle). Background shows butt adapter in place, before the cord is cut off.

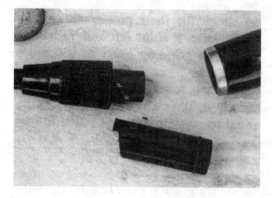

Damage to a rod from breakage of a butt adapter. The fault is not with the butt adapter—the rod blank was not inserted completely into the butt adapter when the rod was built by a custom rod builder. Replacement is easy by splitting off the adapter and adding a new one.

best results use a 24-hour epoxy glue. Slide the ferrule in place, wipe excess glue from the blank or ferrule, and use a razor blade to trim excess shim threads.

Repeat with the male ferrule, seating it all the way on the rod blank. When the glue is cured, finish it off with a thread wrap that begins on the blank and runs slightly onto the ferrule. Use the same color of thread as used on the guide wraps, and coat with an epoxy finish.

Collets for offshore rods and butt adapters or ferrules for detachable-handle casting and popping rods can be shimmed and repaired the same way. The difference is that you will be dealing with the male fitting that will go into a reel seat or rod handle.

Bamboo rods can be repaired this way, too, but there are some additional factors. Some older bamboo rods have a small pin driven through the ferrule and the rod. The ferrule cannot be taken off unless this pin is removed. To remove it, use a small punch or drift (a small nail set works well) to drive it out.

The hexagonal shape of split-bamboo rods also does not conform to the round shape of ferrules. You can use a larger ferrule and slip it over the rod blank, slightly crimping its end to match the flat surfaces of the hexagonal rod blank.

A second method is to use a key-tightened three-jaw chuck in two different positions to form the fitted section of the ferrule into the hexagonal shape of the rod. Both of these methods preserve rod strength because no bamboo skin is cut or removed. The strength of any bamboo rod is primarily in the skin.

Another method involves trimming the corners of the hexagonal rod in the area of the ferrule so that the round ferrule will exactly, or more closely, fit the rod blank. This also keeps the ferrule from looking too bulky, and is easier to trim-wrap with thread. It does weaken the rod slightly, though, because some of the bamboo skin is removed.

Reel Repair

REEL REPAIRS can be simple or extensive, depending upon the degree of wear or damage. Repairs should only be done if you feel confident of your ability to dismantle and reassemble the parts necessary for the repair required. Some tackle manufacturers, warranty centers, and reel repair service centers caution against fishermen repairing reels. This is self-serving to a degree, but it does point out the necessity of care in any reel repairs. This does not mean, however, that reel repairs are difficult.

Some reel repairs are nothing more than a quick replacement of a part, and might almost constitute part of a maintenance program instead of reel repair. Such might be the case with replacing rollers on spinning-reel bails, bail springs, pawls on casting reels, and click drags on fly reels. However, they are replaced because they are worn or damaged, and technically constitute repairs.

If there are any rules when repairing reels they are these:

1. Work on one reel at a time.
2. Make sure the reel is clean and free of grease or grime so you can see what you are doing and how the parts fit and mesh.
3. Have a good work area and a compartmented box to hold parts as you remove them.
4. Pay particular attention to shims, small washers, small springs, and so on to check for their proper reassembly order. This is critical because a shim left out or in the wrong position may result in grinding gears or too much play in part of a reel.
5. Work from left to right when removing parts so that replacement is automatically in the right order.
6. Consult the reel's manual so you can examine parts, fittings of parts, and the part number if you need to order an item.
7. Have the necessary tools and replacement parts before you start. An exception here might be when you know the reel is damaged, but you do not know which parts you need to fix it. Make sure that you can leave the reel disassembled, with the removed parts in order, while you buy or mail-order the required replacements, or that you reassemble the reel after determining what will be required.

It is very important to remove most of the grease from reel housings and gear-

The need for proper care is evidenced in these reels, now completely ruined. The left and center reel have corrosion built up under the side-plate frame and the line guide. A properly cared-for reel is shown on the right.

ings. Failure to do so will prevent you from seeing the small parts and how they fit. And since every reel is a little different, it is important to proceed slowly and to examine the reel parts carefully as you remove them so that you can see how they all fit together.

Before beginning on some basic replacements and repairs, it should be noted there are probably exceptions to the information on fittings, screw positions, gearings, and access to parts. The following, however, should apply to most reels.

Spinning Reels

Roller Replacement The rollers on a spinning-reel bail prevent the line wear that would occur if running over a nonmoving part. The line makes a right-angle bend at this point, turning at right angles as the bail lays the line on the spool. Roller replacement does not require removing the bail. All rollers are held in place by a screw at the end of the bail arm, where the bail wire attaches to the bail arm support.

Loosen this screw and remove it, holding the bail at the same time so no small parts will be lost. Assembly might be as simple as a screw holding the roller in place on the end of the bail wire arm, or might include a bushing under the roller, lock washer under the screw, and bail collar.

Once the screw is off, remove the roller and bushing and replace. If replacement is not required, clean and oil as described in chapter 3, Reel Maintenance.

Bail Assembly Bail assemblies are high on the list of broken parts of spinning reels, according to a poll taken of spinning-reel manufacturers. This is not a design or manufacturing fault. These arms are vulnerable because they are exposed. Dropping a reel can break or bend a bail arm. Bail terminology will vary with each manufacturer, but the bail assembly includes a bail arm attached to one side of the reel rotor (the rotating framework immediately behind the spool that holds the bail and moves it around the spool), with the other end holding the roller and attached to an arm or arm lever assembly. Both of these are held in place with screws.

The screw attachment can go directly through the end of the bail arm into the rotor housing, or be on a separate plate attached to the rotor housing. The lever arm holding the roller end of the bail is held in place with a screw, but a plate arm hides the springs and levers that hold the cocked (open) bail in place until the bail release closes the bail.

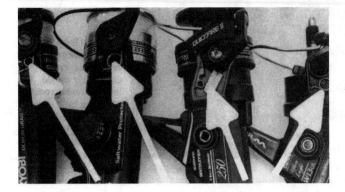

Bail springs most commonly require replacement and repair in spinning reels. These can vary from compression springs to lever springs. Springs are shown on these four spinning reels (arrows pointing to springs).

If the bail is bent, remove the bail arm by unscrewing it at the rotor attachment and at the roller. Remove the bail, and carefully bend it into its original shape. Check the shape to make sure that it will fit back into place without more bending, twisting, or stressing. Reattach and open and close the bail to ensure it works properly.

If a bail spring is broken, the first job is finding it on the reel. Most are directly under the plate covering the arm lever. On older reels that do not feature skirted spools, these were often positioned inside the rotating cup. Once you locate the spring, remove it carefully. The spring is under tension, so you must hold it with small needle-nose pliers or tweezers to prevent it from flying off. If this is impossible, hold your thumb or finger over the spring and pry out one end to release the tension. Then carefully lift the spring out.

If the spring is broken you won't have this problem. Just lift it out and put in a new spring. Use the same cautions for seating the new spring, because the spring must go in under tension. Hold your thumb or finger over the spring and lever or pry one end into place. If a tension spring, such as found on older reels, hook one end in place, hold that end, and lever the other end of the hook into position.

Once the spring is in place, replace the cover and reassemble the arm lever and bail.

Handle Handles also break when reels are dropped or handled roughly. Most spinning-reel handles are easy to replace because they are detachable. Handles are made in two ways. In one, the handle is on a square or hex shaft, which slides through a fitted socket and is held in place with a screw fitting and cap on the opposite side of the reel. The other handle uses two sets of threads on the reel shaft. The handle is backed up to unscrew the shaft from the side housing, and replaced on the opposite side. A small screw-on cap covers the open side to prevent water or dirt intrusion.

Gears Most gears are easy to replace once you open the reel's side plate. The side plate is removed by first taking off the handle. Then loosen the small screws around the perimeter of the housing and lift them off. In most cases these small screws (two or four of them) are the same size and length. If not, note the position of each screw for proper reassembly.

Once you remove the side plate, the gears are fully exposed. If the gears are binding, rough, or grinding, they will have to be replaced. (Be sure, however, that this is not the result of rough, corroded, or damaged bushings or ball bearings.) In most cases, the drive gear is easily taken out for replacement. If the drive shaft containing the pinion gear is damaged, it is necessary to remove the main drive shaft by removing the spool from the reel, loosening the main nut surrounding the shaft, and removing the rotor. This will usually make it possible to slide out the main shaft. Most reels have additional gearing in the main housing to allow for the reciprocal (back-and-forth) motion of the main shaft. This allows the roller on the bail to lay the line down evenly over the spool. If this is attached to the main shaft, it must be removed so this shaft and pinion gearing can be replaced.

On most reels, the shaft is separate from the pinion gear. Removing the spool rotor and the shaft exposes the cover that holds the pinion gear in place. This cover must be taken off to remove and replace the pinion gear.

Whether this is necessary or not will depend upon the reel's care, usage, and construction. Inexpensive reels with zinc or low-quality gearings will require replacement in time. Those with high-quality, cut stainless-steel or brass gearing will last a long time and, with care, maybe a lifetime. Reels not cared for or lubed regularly and properly can also wear, regardless of the gear construction. In most cases, this extensive a dismantling of the reel will not be necessary except under extreme circumstances.

Once the parts are removed, grease and oil them as per the manufacturer's instructions and replace in exact reverse order in which they were removed.

Drags Drags on spinning reels are in either the spool or rear housing (as in rear-drag reels). All reels that are fished heavily for big fish will ultimately require drag replacement. Spinning-reel drags in the spool are easy to replace. First remove the spool. Most reel drags have a small spring-retaining ring to hold the drag washers in place. Use pliers or a small screwdriver to pry the spring out, holding your thumb over the spring to prevent loss. Once this is removed, the drag washers slide out.

These are alternately hard and soft washers, with the hard metal washers alternately keyed to the spool and the shaft. This is how the drag works. Pressure on the drag through the drag-adjustment knob creates friction in the drag. The hard washers keyed to the shaft stay stationary while those keyed to the spool rotate. The soft washers between them keep the drag running smoothly while the pressure on the drag controls the degree of breaking power used in the drag.

Multidisc drags, as these are often called, will have, in order: a hard washer keyed to the spool, a soft washer, a hard washer keyed to the shaft, a soft washer, a hard washer keyed to the spool, and so on. Some drags also have a spring at the bottom to help control the pressure and provide more drag control.

In these drag systems, as in any such system, only the soft or fiber washers are changed or replaced. Hard metal washers normally never need replacing. Metal washers can be washed and polished, but do not use steel wool or sandpaper because they will abrade the surface and make the drag rough acting.

When replacing a drag system, check with the manufacturer or reel manual for oiling instructions. Some drags use a light oil, while others should never be oiled. Ignoring this can be critical in how and how well the drag works.

Other types of spool drags are being developed. Some manufacturers are eliminating small multidisc drag systems and going to large single-disc drag features. These can be on top of the spool, or under the spool, as in some Fin-Nor spinning reels. These are no more difficult to reach, only different. A small retainer ring usually holds these drag systems in place. Removing the retaining ring exposes the drag washer or washers. The main difference is that there is usually only one hard and one soft washer. This does not mean that these drags are inferior because they lack parts—some of the finest reels in the world use similar systems. The larger washer spreads the breaking over a bigger area to better dissipate the heat buildup caused by friction. These are usually far smoother reel drags.

Drags in the rear of the reel housing (rear drags) are more difficult to reach, and often vary more widely in construction with reel manufacturers. To expose and replace these soft washers, remove the handle and the side plate as above. To remove the washers you must fully extend the shaft. This is easy to do before removing the handle or after removing the side plate by inserting and turning the handle in the reel socket. You will have to remove the rear drag control. In some reels this is held in place with a U-shaped retaining ring, which prevents removing the drag knob. Remove this, and the drag knob can be completely unscrewed. An alternative method uses a screw to hold the drag knob on from the rear. Remove this and the knob comes off. Once the knob is off, the washers can be exposed and removed. Some can be lifted out of the side of the reel, while others come off the back, after removing a retaining ring that holds them in place like the spool-drag washers.

Replace the soft washers, oil if called for, replace the drag assembly in the reel, and reassemble in order.

Some reels have a front spool-operated drag system in combination with a light-pressure rear system. This is used to control line taken by a fish when bait fishing. Two examples are Shimano's Baitrunner system and Silstar's Baitfeeder. In both cases, the rear drag exerts only very light pressure on the line when a fish takes bait. These operate as a drag on the spool shaft with the main drag working with the shaft stationary and against the spool drag. These rear controls are just like any rear drag in construction and replacement of washers.

Other Parts Most other reel parts are readily accessible. The only other part of spinning reels is the antireverse click. This might be as simple as a lever with a leaf spring, or as complicated as a silent antireverse system. Rarely do these need replacement, and all are easily reached and repaired, either in the reel housing or underneath the spool rotor.

Spincast Reels

Spincast-reel gearing is similar to that on spinning reels, though simpler.

Handles Handles break in falls just as they do on spinning reels. Replacement is simple, because most handles are held on the shaft with a screw or nut. Unscrew to remove the broken handle and replace with a new one.

Gears Gears are reached in one of two ways. On some reels the reel's entire working mechanism comes out of the housing when you remove the nose cone. Remove the nose cone by turning it counterclockwise to remove screw attachments, turn counterclockwise for about ½ inch to remove those with a lock-on bayonet mount. Pull out the gearing/handle parts. The gearing will be visible from the rear, where it can be lubricated or checked for wear and replacement. Other reels feature access through the side plate, just as with spinning reels. As with spinning reels, you must first remove the handle, then the star drag (turn counterclockwise). Remove the screws in the side plate to lift it off and expose the gearing.

Some shafts holding the main drive gear are free and can be slipped off for replacement, though others require removing other parts or brackets to get the gear loose. A bracket usually holds the central shaft and pinion gear in place; removal of the bracket or other parts will allow replacement of the shaft and gear.

Spool To take off the spool, first remove the nose cone. Remove the winding cup—the protective cone under the nose cone that holds the pickup pin, which retrieves line—by turning it counterclockwise.

Once the winding cup is removed, the spool is exposed and can usually be slipped off, though others require removing other brackets and retaining features before removing and checking.

Pickup Pin It is also possible to check the pickup pin on the underside of the winding cup when you look at the spool. Pins operate on a cam or spring system and are easy to check or replace if worn.

Snubber or Line Brake The snubber or line brake, which holds the line when casting or slowing at the end of the cast, is on the outside (front) of the winding cup. It may be hard rubber or plastic. It can sometimes separate from the winding cup and cause problems. To repair this, use a good flexible rubber cement or epoxy to recement the snubber. If the snubber is worn or brittle and cracked, pry it off and replace with a new one.

Drag The drag on spincast reels works and looks like those on casting reels. The star drag on some spincast reels is under the handle and consists of pressure plates that compress soft or fiber washers to create the friction on line pulled from the reel. (Metal pressure plates alternating with soft washers are basic to any drag system, however.)

To check or replace the washer, remove the star drag wheel by turning it counterclockwise. Then remove, in turn and with close attention to their position, each of the successive washers, shims, plates, springs, and other mechanisms. Replace the soft or fiber washers if required and reassemble.

Fly Reels

Most fly reels are simple, with some consisting of no more than a half-dozen main parts and a few screws. Most damage to fly reels results when they've been

The rim overlapping feature makes rim-control fly reels far more susceptible to damage. Sometimes they can be bent back into shape. Here a small pair of pliers is being used to bend out a rim-control spool. The strip of cardboard protects the reel from damage.

dropped and the frame or spool has been bent. The frame or spool may be bent back into shape, but this may crack the part, because these reels are often hard-tempered aluminum alloys. If they are plastic or cast metal, they usually can't be rebent to their original shape and will crack.

To rebend a bent spool or frame (you have nothing to lose, since with a bent part the reel can't be used anyway), use pliers with the jaws wrapped with several layers of masking tape to avoid marring the reel. Bend gently and slowly, and check periodically for clearance. Do not bend more than is absolutely necessary for clearance, because this might crack the reel.

Handles Dropping reels can bend the handles. Some handles are riveted on the spool so replacement is impossible. Try to bend the handle back in place. If the handle can be removed, replace it with a new one.

Line Guards Line guards are those small, hard brackets that are designed to protect the line from wear when it is pulled off the reel when casting. These are usually easily replaced. You may have to dismantle the reel on models in which this part slides into place under a framing plate.

Clicks and Drags Most fly reels have simple clicks and drag mechanisms. On most reels, these are under the spool, on the inside of the frame. They vary widely in design. Some have large pressure-plate drags, a fine example of which would be the Fin-Nor fly reel. Others have small cam-control click drags or combination click and pressure drags. The better pressure-plate drag systems are on large saltwater and salmon-sized fly reels (which need them), while most other reels have small click drags.

Casting Reels

Before removing the left side plate on magnetic casting reels, it is *very important* to check your reel manual. Some of the controls are geared and spring loaded. Failure to place the setting to that indicated by the reel manual may result in the magnetic control not setting correctly when reassembled, and not working properly!

Old pawl has been removed and a new one is ready to be inserted into the reel.

This usually means setting the controls on 10 or the maximum setting, because this is the position at which the north/south magnets in two concentric rings will automatically position themselves. But check the reel manual!

Pawl These are small toothlike pins that control the back-and-forth movement of the levelwind. They are easy to replace. Use a screwdriver or reel tool to remove the cap on the underside of the levelwind mechanism. Pull out the pawl and replace. These are usually supplied in a small bottle of parts that comes with the reel. Pawls should be regularly checked.

Worm Gear The worm gear is the crisscross gearing in which the pawl rides. It makes it possible for the pawl carrying the levelwind to move back and forth and evenly place line on the spool. Worm gears also wear and, in time, require replacement. Removing and replacing them is possible from either the right or left side of the plate, which varies with the reel manufacturer.

Some levelwind worm gears slide out after the pawl has been removed, when the right or left side plate is removed. Others have a small retaining ring holding the worm gear in place, while still others are held by small locking brackets that must be slipped off before removing the worm gear.

Handle Handles can break or bend during falls and knocks. They are easy to replace. Most are fastened with a nut that, in turn, is held in place with a locking washer (handle nut-locking plate) and screw. Remove this, then loosen and remove the nut. Some handles have an additional screw in the end of the shaft under the nut. This also must be removed before taking off the handle.

Once the handle is removed, the drag can also be adjusted, cleaned, or replaced.

Drag Remove the handle as above. Then unscrew the star drag control counterclockwise. Remove the screws that hold the side plate onto the base plate (on which the gears, antireverse, and free-spool mechanisms are secured) and remove the side plate. Lift out the bearing spacer, drag-spring washers, drag washers, spacers, pressure plates, and other parts. These must be removed in order and kept in order for proper reassembly. Replace the soft drag washers if required and reassemble.

Casting reel with, left to right, main gear, drag washer, antireverse plate, spacers, and pinion gear.

Spinning-reel drags on front-drag systems are almost always found in the spool. These typical drags are examples from three reels. Note that the soft and hard (metal) washers alternate and that spring clips hold all of them in place. The hard washers alternately have "ears" to engage the spool and a square hole to engage the shaft of the reel. The pressure between these two parts creates the braking or slipping action of the drag.

Pinion and Main Gears These are on the handle side of the reel. The main gear is attached to the handle shaft and turns the pinion gear. The size and number of teeth in each gear determine the gear ratio, for example, 4:1, 6.1:1, and so on. The teeth can be checked and replaced when the handle and side plate are removed (see above). In most cases the drive gear (along with the drag system previously mentioned) is on one main shaft and can be lifted out and examined or replaced.

Other Parts Make sure all other parts are in place during reassembly. These include click alarms, antireverse pawls, flipping controls, and so on. Many of these operate on a spring or lever mechanism to change the on/off controls in these systems. As casting reels become more complicated, more attention must be given to these parts. Check the reel manual for specific details on proper positioning of parts.

Conventional Offshore and Boat Reels

These are nothing more than large rotary-spool reels and resemble sturdy, simple casting reels. They usually contain click alarms, but lack the levelwind, flipping

New gearing in place on casting reel. The main gear also hides the drag washer. Spacers are on the shaft that the handle fastens to and the pinion gear is also shown.

feature, magnetic cast control, free-spool cast control, and similar appointments that are on small freshwater casting models.

Some simple repair suggestions follow, but casting-reel instructions should also be consulted.

Handle These are usually locked in place with a handle lock plate, which must be removed. Handles are easily replaced on big-game reels.

Pinion and Main Gears These are under the handle (right) side plate. Remove the handle and the star drag wheel. Remove all the screws around the perimeter of the reel. Keep these in order, because some screws might be different lengths. Remove the side plate. Undo the smaller screws in the side plate that will allow removal and exposure of the main and pinion gears. Most of these gearing systems are simple and easy to replace, especially when compared to smaller casting reels. Pay careful attention when removing screws to prevent parts from falling out, which will make replacement positions difficult to determine. Check, replace needed parts, and reassemble.

Drag The drag is similar, although heavier, than that of a casting reel. It is directly under the star drag wheel. All screws must usually be removed to expose the drag so soft washers may be replaced. Replace the washers and reassemble.

After you have repaired and reassembled any reel, check it out thoroughly to be sure it works properly. This is just like the trip check listed in chapter 3 to ensure that the reel is completely functional. If something is not right or if reassembly was incorrect, you want to know it now, not when you are out on the water.

Exposed gearing on a casting reel.

CHAPTER

Lure Repair

L
URES ARE SELDOM thought of as fishing tackle that is repaired. As their cost has gone up, however, so has the interest in keeping them serviceable and repairing them when possible. Many repair basics apply to many lures, so generic repairs will be covered first, followed by a short section on repairs for each type of lure.

Hook Replacement

Hooks can be replaced on most lures. In many lures, such as crankbaits, plugs, top-water lures, structure spoons, spinners, trolling lures, in-line spinnerbaits, or weight-forward spinners, the single, double, or treble hooks are free swinging. If hooks are attached by split rings, repair is simple. Open the split ring, preferably with split-ring pliers, and remove the damaged, broken, or rusted hook. Once you begin to remove the hook, and have the split ring spread, you can slide the new hook on with the same motion.

If the hook is attached to the lure with a wire ring, as on a spinner, or with a molded-in hook hanger, as on some plugs, cut the hook eye (*not* the hook hanger) and remove it, replacing it with hooks on split rings. One problem that sometimes develops with plugs is that the split ring adds length to the hook so that the several hooks on a plug can catch together.

If this occurs, there are two solutions. One is to buy short-shank hooks (they are made in single and treble hooks); the other is to buy an open-eye hook, such as an open-eye Siwash salmon single hook or open-eye treble. When closed with pliers, the hooks are sufficiently strong.

Trolling spoons often have single fixed hooks that are fastened to the spoon blade by a pop-type rivet or bolt and nut. They are easy to replace, but generally you must use the same style and size of hook as the original, to conform to the bend and shape of the lure.

Hooks on standard spinnerbaits, jigs, buzzbaits, and trolling or weed spoons with welded hooks cannot be easily removed and replaced. If you are adept with soldering and welding equipment, you may consider removing hooks from fixed-hook trolling and weedless spoons and resoldering new ones in their place.

Repainting, Recoating, and Polishing Lure Bodies

Almost all lures can be repainted. This is easier than ever, particularly because some companies have introduced paints just for lures. Both hobby paint companies and tackle companies have introduced such paints. These paints can be used on all lures. They are hard, quick-drying, high-gloss, waterproof paints. They can be used either in the home workshop for detailed refurbishing, or for quick color changes of lures when fishing.

When making quick color changes with these paints, make sure the lure is dry, and repaint it in the shade. If finishing in the bright sun, turn so your body shades the lure. The shade lengthens the curing time, which is important because these paints set up in seconds. The best technique is to first design a pattern or pick a color and use the applicator brush fastened to the cap to rapidly apply the paint. Avoid going over the paint repeatedly.

There are some portable spray systems, which are different from the brush systems above. These systems use a sprayer nozzle that connects with tubing to a master aerosol air propellent. This propellent sprays the paint on the lure, where it instantly dries. It will not wash off with water. Simple kits that operate from aerosol cans are available from art and hobby shops.

There are several techniques for repainting lures at home under more controlled conditions. The brush-applicator/quick-dry paints work well and provide bright colors. They are best used when painting a lure one color or when repainting lures with several contrasting blocks or bands of color. (Many fishing-lure manufacturers believe that hard contrasting colors make the best-attracting lures.)

Methods of painting lures include:

1. Brushing: Best for quick-drying acrylic paints. Some paints, like those from Testor's, have a built-in felt tip for painting lures. In both cases, apply sparingly, evenly, and rapidly; avoid repeating brush strokes over the same area. Slower-drying paints should be applied the same way, although some overlapping is possible.

2. Dipping: Dipping works best with thin paints. Apply repeated coats and dip slowly to prevent runs, sags, and drips from curing on the lure. Use a long trough for the paint and line up the lures in holders. Dip all the lures and hang them over the paint so that the lure bottom barely touches the paint. This allows rapid runoff of excess paint, after which the rack of lures can be hung to dry. It is important to keep the level of the paint in the trough constant to allow runoff to occur, and to use the same-sized lures.

    In cases where this is too slow, hang the lure rack, then later blot the bottom of each lure to remove excess paint. Dipping is most effective on jig, spinnerbait, and buzzbait heads before the tails are attached.

3. Spraying: This is only possible with aerosol enamels or lacquers. It's not widely used because it is messy and wastes paint. It can produce good results, though. One possibility is to spray a light color, such as white, cream, or yellow, on a crankbait belly with one pass of color; follow with a streak of side color (green, red, blue, tan, silver are popular); and finish with a strip along the back in black, dark brown, or dark blue/green. The result is

a natural-looking, professionally finished plug with a color pattern similar to that of a live baitfish or minnow.

For an added touch, wrapping the sides in scale netting before painting will produce a scale finish. Each spray of paint must be allowed to dry or cure before the next is applied. Painting many lures with the same color scheme maximizes efficiency and minimizes paint waste.

When spray painting, it helps to use a special painting box to contain the airborne paint. You can use an open cardboard box, with the open end on the side, and line the box with cloth scraps, cotton batting, or sponges. These will capture and hold the spray.

Most spoons are polished, and those that have lost their gleam can be painted to give them new life. For this, scrub the spoon with steel wool to remove any dirt, rust, or corrosion. Then mask the hook, line tie, weedguard, and so on that you do not want to paint with tape. Dip or spray with an anti-rust primer, allow to dry, then finish with two coats of enamel or other lure paint. If using light colors, first apply a white base coat. Many primers are dark, and light-colored paints will not adequately cover dark colors.

You can repaint lures when you are afield. Hold them carefully or grip them with finishing pliers and use the paintbrush cap to completely coat any lure. If you like to paint each lure individually, use disposable plastic gloves to keep your hands clean.

When repainting and refinishing lures at the end of the season, set up an assembly-line system. Use a rack to cure many freshly sprayed or dipped lures. Depending upon the lure type, one possibility is a wide U-shaped wooden rack with a hanger across the top. Use hangers of bead chain, standard small-link chain, or pipe strap (a flexible strap with holes every few inches, from which lure hooks can be hung), which will prevent lures from sliding and touching.

Repainting can include applying special patterns. Two of these are scale netting and stencils.

Scale netting comes in several sizes and patterns from lure part companies. Veiling or tulle, found in any fabric store, can be a good substitute. Try to find a coarse material with spacing suitable to the scale pattern you want to create.

There are two ways to use netting. One is to hold the lure, with the scale net-

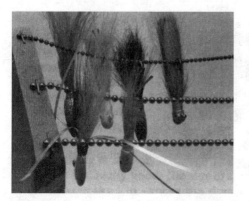

All painted lures must be hung up to dry after painting. Use special racks of bead chain (as shown), strap iron (which has holes to separate the lures), or regular chain. These keep the lures separated. Plain cord or wire will sag and the lures will all slide together.

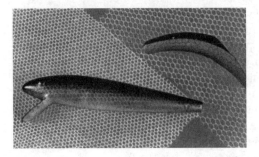

Old lures can be made to look as good as new ones by spray painting them through scale nettings (tulle, available at fabric stores, also works well). Examples of scale netting and painted lures.

ting wrapped securely around it, and spray the side of the lure. When working this way, paint a number of lures by spraying one side, letting the paint cure, then spraying the other side.

A second way to do this is to mount the scale netting loosely in an open frame. Press the lure against the netting, spray it, then turn it over to spray the other side. To prevent damage to the still-wet finish on the first side, mount the lure body on a nail held by a pair of pliers or, if working with a spinnerbait head or jig head, hold the hook with pliers. Another possibility is to lay the lure body on a foam pad, push the frame with the loose netting on top of it, and spray straight down. Lift the frame, carefully remove the lure so the fresh paint won't be damaged, and replace with another lure body. Do one side of a number of lures, allow them to cure, and repeat on the second side.

An embroidery hoop, designed to hold fabric tightly, is ideal for holding scale netting. They come in sizes ranging from about 3 to 24 inches in diameter. If you are really serious about this method of repainting, check silkscreen and printing supply houses and needlework mail-order firms for special hinges that fasten hoop and rectangular frames to a worktable for productionlike work. Lacking this, other hinges could be fastened permanently to a net scale frame.

Stencils are cutout patterns that protect the areas you don't want painted. (We all used stencils in school to outline letters for projects.) Stencils with wavy patterns, spots and dots, scalelike cutouts, and other designs are available from art supply stores.

You can also make stencils by cutting a pattern from sheeting with fine scissors. Paper or cardboard can be used for such templates, but I prefer clear, stiff plas-

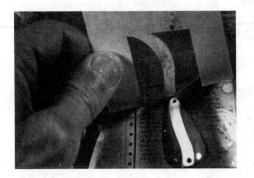

Old lures can be painted using templates to add stripes or spots. Templates can be easily cut from cardboard or lightweight plastic.

tic—the kind used for term paper covers. It is easy to cut, and the clear sheeting allows for proper placement over the lure (until the stencil is covered with paint). Cleaning off the paint after each session keeps these stencils clear enough for long-term use. Stencils can be used in two ways. If you want a hard line of sprayed color, keep the stencil in contact with the lure. For a diffused line, keep the stencil about ¼ to ½ inch away. Experiment for the best results.

Heavily rusted lures can also be painted, first removing any roughness and sealing with a primer coat before painting.

Rubber Coating Rubber or plastic-dip coatings are ideal for refinishing and repairing some lures. These coatings are solvent based so that they are water-proof, and are really designed for coating tool handles such as pliers, hammers, wire cutters, and so on. They can be bought from specialty hardware supply houses such as Brookstone, in some better hardware stores, and through industrial tool distributors. You won't find a variety of hues, but you should have no problem locating basic colors such as red, green, yellow, white, black, blue, and orange. The stuff is expensive, because it comes in about 8-ounce cans that cost $6 to $8 each. The coatings are designed for slow dipping, and are ideal for lures such as jigs and stripped spinnerbait or buzzbait heads. A spray-type coating is also available, but would be wasteful because the lures are so small.

Dyeing Lures can also be dyed. Sometimes this finish looks almost like a new paint job. In most cases, though, it results in a translucent overlay of color through which a base color can be seen. Dyes available include everything from those used in per-manent felt-tip markers, shoe dyes, clothes dyes such as Rit and Tintex, and those specifically made for lures, available from several companies. Technically, a dye col-ors an object by saturating it with a coloring solution. Dyes are also described as coloring with a hue or tint of a color, which would apply to the uses described above. The main difference between paint and dye is the visible coating left on products by the former.

Soft and hard lures can be colored with dye. Soft lures such as fur, feather, syn-thetic products, rubber, and vinyl plastics absorb the coloring. Hard lures such as jig heads, spoons, plastic crankbaits, and painted wood lures take on a hue or tint of color when the dye solvent evaporates. Dyes usually dry more slowly than the quick-dry paints, but far faster than standard paints.

Hard lures, such as jig heads, spinnerbaits, spoons, spinners, and so on are best when dyed a light color. White is the only base color that will take a true dye color. Dyes are best applied by dipping.

Polishing Metal lures can easily and quickly become tarnished and dull, which will deter their ability to catch fish. To correct for this, polish the lures to restore them back or close to their original luster. Methods of polishing include:

1. Metal polishes: Polishes for silver, brass, and copper will all work well. Brands such as Flitz, Brasso, Twinkle, Oneida, and so on are all good. On high-sheen lures, which might be scratched by these cleaners, use fiberglass

polish or Chrome Foam, used by photographers for cleaning and polishing ferrotype plates. In most cases, however, standard metal finishes are okay.

2. Colas: Colas (that's right—the kind you drink) are often used to remove corrosion from metal lures. If there is heavy finish damage, soak the lure overnight. Often this will be enough, but be sure to wash the lure after soaking.

3. Abrasives: Dirt or fine sand is an abrasive you can use afield, though it might scratch the finish. Obviously, scratches are less important than catching fish, so this is a minor disadvantage.

Cigarette and cigar ashes are also finely abrasive. When wet and rubbed on a lure, they also provide a quick field fix.

A small piece of emery cloth carried in a tacklebox or field repair kit (see chapter 10) helps to polish any metal lure. Unlike sandpaper, which is on a paper base that will be damaged by moisture, emery cloth is on a fabric base. It can be used for a long time without losing its abrasiveness.

Spoons that cannot be restored by polishing can be repainted.

Re-Forming Lures

Metal lures can bend during fishing. Strong fish, casts into rocks, snags, and stuffing lures into tacklebox compartments all can cause bending and damage. Most damage involves light-wire lures such as spinners, spinnerbaits, and buzzbaits, but spoons, jigs, metal plates, and props on crankbaits and topwater lures are not immune to abuse. Wires, plates, and props are often easily bent back into shape with pliers. Spring wire is often used on these lures, so you usually will have to bend the wire past the point desired, and allow it to spring back to the original position.

Light, thin, metal spoons can also get bent and be rebent into their original position with pliers. Lure hooks can be bent out of shape from fish and snags. Hooks are tempered wire, so take care when bending them back into shape. Hold the lure carefully, grip the hook point with parallel-action fishing pliers or vise-grip pliers for added strength, and, taking care not to bend the barb, slowly and evenly bend the hook back into position.

Remelting Lures

Soft-plastic lures can be remelted or heat-treated to repair minor tears and abrasion. Save old worms and soft lures instead of throwing them away so that they can be reused. This involves not so much repairing old lures as making new ones out of the old.

Some possibilities include:

1. Take a worm with a damaged or torn head, cut off the damaged portion, and heat it with a flame to round off the head into a new, shorter lure.

2. Remove the damaged tail from one worm and the damaged head from another. Join the salvageable parts by heating the ends in a flame.

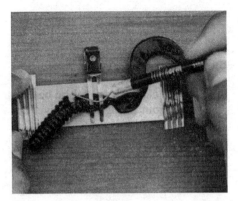

This tool was made specifically for rewelding plastic worms. The clamps hold the worm in place, the heating tool plugs into a 12-volt cigarette lighter and heats the worm to weld it. The same thing can be done at home using an AC welder or macramé cord-cutting tool.

3. Remove salvageable curly tails from damaged worms and join them side by side with a flame to make double spinnerbait, buzzbait, spoon, or jig tails.
4. Remove salvageable tails from worms and use heat to adhere them to the sides of worms to make lizards and salamanders.
5. Use heat to add curly worm tails to soft minnows and fish to make eels.
6. Do all of the above in contrasting color parts to make different lures than those commercially available.

Using a flame is not difficult, but you must take care because molten plastic can burn (soft lure plastic usually melts at about 375°F). For best results, use a disposable lighter, which burns cleaner than other flames. Any flame will work, but unclean flames or too high a heat will burn and dirty the plastic.

Have a fishing buddy hold the lighter as you use both hands to hold the parts close to the flame. This way both parts are heated at the same time and a stronger joint will be formed when they are joined. Cooling is almost immediate, so that you can fish with the new lures seconds after making them. If you don't have a friend to hold the lighter, consider buying a standard lighter that will stay on unattended when lit. That way you can sit the lighter on a boat seat or picnic bench and hold the plastic parts in the flame.

For cleanest results, hold the parts to be joined to the side of the flame, not directly over it. The result is more evenly controlled heat and less danger of burning and discoloring.

Gluing

Many plugs, crankbaits, and topwater lures are made of hollow plastic. As a result, these lures can open along a seam line or crack when they hit rocks or are struck by a toothy fish. Cracks often can be repaired with an instant glue or five-minute epoxy. First make sure the lure is completely dry. If it has been recently fished, you may have to open the crack with a toothpick to drain the water.

When it is dry, leave the toothpick in place and use a second toothpick to spread glue on the joining edges of the crack. Remove the toothpick, hold the lure firmly to squeeze these parts together, and use a paper towel to remove excess glue.

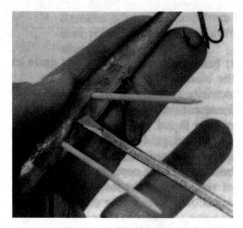

Split or cracked crankbaits (hollow injection-molded plastic lures) can be repaired by regluing them. The crack on this hollow lure is held open with toothpicks. The screwdriver blade helps to get the toothpicks into the crack. The toothpicks should be at the end of the split to hold it open for gluing.

Hold the lure together until the glue is dry, which will take only seconds with an instant glue and no more than a few minutes for a five-minute epoxy. If using a long-curing glue, hold the lure under constant pressure with a carpenter's spring clamp.

You might have to glue metal wobbling plates into a crankbait or topwater plug when they become loose. Remove the plate, which is usually held in place with tiny screws, add glue to the holes (looseness often results from enlarged holes that are too big to hold the screws), add glue to any other necessary contact parts, replace the plates, and screw them in place.

If the damage is extensive, you may have to replace the screws with longer ones (available from tackle supply houses), but be careful so you do not penetrate a lure's hollow body. If this is a possibility, force more glue into the hole so that the combination of screw and glue will seal any opening.

Refinishing Metal Parts Metal lure parts such as spoons, spinner blades, buzzbait blades, metal wobbling plates, spinner bodies, and so on can be repaired with metal refinishing or replating kits available at craft and hobby shops. While this is fun, it's not often economically wise, because the kits can be far more expensive than replacing the blades.

Most kits work on electricity (battery or AC). Metal is replated by running a small current through the part when coating or soaking it with a refinishing liquid. Available finishes include nickel, copper, brass, silver, and gold. In most cases, nickel, copper, and brass finishes can be used on any metal. Gold and silver finishes can only be applied over copper or brass plating.

The main advantage of replating is that the blades on rigged lures, such as spinner blades on a long-leader cowbell rig, can be refinished without removing them from the rig.

Retying Tails

Many lures have tied-in tails of feathers, fur, or synthetic fur. These include spoons, topwater lures, and crankbaits, with tails on the tail hook; jigs, spinnerbaits, and buzzbaits, with tails on the hook shank or collar; and saltwater hose lures and spinners, which have tails tied on the hook.

To repair these, use a razor blade or sharp knife to cut off all the old fur or feathers and the thread holding it in place. Clamp the hook or lure in a vise. A fly-tying vise is preferable, but lacking that vise grips will do if they are mounted on a workbench or held in a workbench vise. Larger lures can be held directly in a workbench vise.

Use fly-tying or rod-building thread (size 2/0 or A for smaller lures, size D on larger ones) to wrap the hook shank or lure part. Be extremely careful to prevent cutting the thread with the hook points. One way to prevent the hook points from cutting the thread is to cover the points with masking tape, tie the lure, then remove the tape when finished. Make several wraps with the thread and trim the tag end. Maintaining tension, wrap in the new fur or feathers.

To wrap in feathers, determine the length of the feather you wish to use and strip off all the hackle, hurl, or feather fibers forward of this point. To tie in fur, clip the fur close to the skin, or fabric base if using fake fur, and hold the fur by the ends. Use a small comb to strip out any underfur that would add bulk (making it difficult to tie) but no action or length to the fur. Cut the skin end of the fur to the length desired.

Lay the fur or feathers over the spot where they will be tied down and wrap them with the thread. For best results, get an even distribution of the fur or feathers around the hook or lure. There are several ways to do this. With treble hooks it is usually best to divide the material into three equal bundles and tie each in place between the two points of the treble hook. Another method, which is ideal for jigs, is to tie in the entire bundle. Loosely wrap the thread three or four times around the body and material. Then pull tight, working the fur or feathers around the body of the lure for even distribution. On larger lures, you may wish to do this in two or more bundles to get a large tail in place.

Once the new tail is secured, clip off excess material forward of the wrap. Then continue wrapping until the cut ends are completely covered. At this point, finish off the wrap using three or four half hitches, binding each of them down into the wrap.

Cut the excess thread and protect the wrap with a coating of paint (this can be done at the same time a lure is dipped to paint the head), epoxy finish (such as that used in rod building), or varnish. For a quick protective coating, several coats of nylon-based clear nail polish work well.

Rebuilding Lures

Some lures can be completely rebuilt. A prime example is a spinner, because all its parts can be removed and used as replacements in other damaged lures, or it can be rebuilt after cleaning, polishing, or repainting. To do this, cut the eye of the spinner shaft at either the line-tie or hook end. (Do this with care, because the cut end will fly off forcefully. Aim this end at a waste container.)

Once this is done, remove the parts and save them. The usual assembly procedure for rebuilding a standard spinnerbait involves working with an eyed shaft. If you do not have access to these, they can be made with round or needle-nose pli-

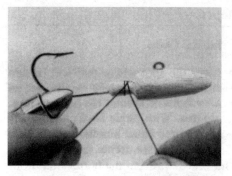

Old jigs can be cut down, repainted with a base coat of white, and retied, as with this lure. Here, thread is being tied in place.

Tail material is being tied down.

Tail material clipped for wrapping collar.

After the collar is wrapped, the tying is finished by wrapping off with half hitches.

ers and .030 wire. Using this eye as the line tie, put the clevis on the spinner blade and then thread the clevis onto the shaft, making sure that the concave side of the blade is next to the shaft.

Continue by adding the body or beads. Once these are in place, form the final eye with the pliers. Before the eye is complete, add the hook, then wrap the eye around the spinner shaft. The eye must be aligned with the spinner shaft and not cocked to one side.

Similar lure rebuilding can be done on spinnerbaits and buzzbaits. Remove the skirts and blades and rebuild them to your own design, or replace damaged or corroded parts.

Rerigging

Some lures are built onto wire or monofilament leaders. The leader is an essential part of the lure, because otherwise the lure cannot be tied to the line. Examples are offshore trolling lures, cowbells or long spinner blades for deep lake trolling, and tandem lures that are connected with monofilament or wire.

When these rigs are damaged, the simple solution is to rerig the lure. The leader on offshore lures can kink badly when fighting a large fish, which makes the leader weak and unsafe to use. On the same lures, the constant skipping on the surface can abrade the leader where it comes through a hole in the lure head. Corrosion, toothy fish, poor storage (which twists or bends leaders), and fighting fish can also damage leaders.

Leaders can't really be repaired or restored, so they must be replaced. Cut off the old leader, taking note of how the leader and lure were originally rigged. Replace the leader with identical material. Leaders have loops for tying on the line or terminal hooks that are tied in knots, made with a haywire twist or formed with leader sleeves and a crimping tool.

To retie, use a perfection loop or figure-eight knot or similar loop that will be aligned with the main leader strand. Practice making haywire twists so they will be done correctly. To make these, loosely twist both wire strands together, finish with a tight wrap around the main strand of wire, then break the excess wire to form a tight loop with no protecting wire end. To do this, form the wire into a small handle, then bend the wire against the completed wire turns to break it by metal fatigue.

To make loops with leader sleeves, use the correct sleeve for the size and type of leader. You only need a simple loop for most leaders, but for offshore leaders, make a compound loop in which the loop is doubled and twisted before the loop end is run back through the sleeve. This creates extra strength in the loop for the heavy strain of this fishing.

Possible repairs for various types of lures include:

1. Topwater lures: Hook replacement, repaint lure body when discolored or damaged, reglue if cracked, refasten and cement wobbling plates or lips.
2. Crankbaits (medium- and deep-diving plugs): Hook replacement, repaint lure body when discolored or damaged, reglue if cracked, refasten and cement wobbling plates or lips.
3. Worms and soft-plastic lures: Smooth damaged worms and soft lures with heat or a flame, make new lures from old ones by joining parts together with heat or flame.
4. Spinners: Polish, refinish, or replace blades, replace hooks, replace tags and skirts, paint bodies, rebuild spinners.
5. Spinnerbaits: Repaint bodies, rubber-coat bodies, straighten wires, replace skirts, refinish blades, polish, re-form, or repaint spinner blades, replace stinger hooks, rebuild spinnerbaits.
6. Buzzbaits: Repaint or rubber-coat bodies, straighten wires, replace skirts, polish, refinish, straighten, or repaint blades, replace stinger hooks, rebuild buzzbaits.
7. Weedless spoons: Rebend spoon blades, straighten or replace hooks (where possible), repaint, refinish, or polish blades.
8. Structure or jigging spoons: Replace hooks, polish, repaint, refinish, or rebend blades.
9. Jigs: Repaint, replace weedguards and skirts, retie tails.
10. Offshore trolling lures: Repaint, replace hooks, rerig, rewrap skirts.

Accessory Repair

A CCESSORIES ENCOMPASS a range of fishing equipment that runs the gamut from landing nets to fishing pliers to waders. Most can be repaired if they are damaged.

Line is not a fishing accessory, but as in chapter 5, Accessory Maintenance, it is discussed first.

Line

While line can't be effectively repaired, broken monofilament can be tied in barrel or blood knots, wire can be spliced by twisting together the two ends, and hollow Dacron can be mended with a splicing needle. The latter involves overlapping the ends, then running each into the hollow center of the other line. In principle, the strength of the splice works like a Chinese finger puzzle. Gel-spun lines must be joined carefully using special knots.

Fly lines can be repaired, to a degree, by splicing the useful line to other parts of lines. Anglers used to do this occasionally to modify lines, such as cutting a double-taper line in half and splicing the two cut ends to half of a level line to, in effect, get two weight-forward tapers. Level lines are far cheaper than double or weight-forward tapers, so the result was two inexpensive lines. Similarly, when a line end is cut or becomes damaged, cracked, or brittle, it can be cut off and discarded, while the remaining line is used to make new lines.

To make a new line, use a knife to strip 1 inch of coating (usually PVC) off the ends of the lines to be joined. Fray out the braided core of line. If possible, separate these strands into two bundles and mate the bundles of the two ends. Evenly wrap these ends with fine fly-tying thread and tie off with half hitches. Then coat the wrap and splice with a flexible glue such as Pliobond.

Fly lines have thin cores that are often difficult to work with, so an alternative is to fold each end over the other so that they are connected (like an open loop) then wrap and finish as above.

In addition to home remedies for lines and loops, there is a number of line-splicing kits, preformed braided loops, glues, and shrink tubing available for working on fly lines.

Fishing Pliers

Broken fishing pliers can't be repaired. Sometimes, though, the slip-on vinyl or rubber handles can be replaced or repaired. There are two simple solutions. One is to remove the old grips and replace them with new ones, which are available at hardware stores. Several sizes are sold; be sure to buy the correct size for your fishing pliers. Soak the grips in hot water to ease sliding them into place. A little soap or hand lotion will also provide lubrication.

Grips can also be dipped into a plastic-coating solution. These are sold in hardware stores in different colors. For best results, make sure that the grips are clean and dry and dip them into the solution several times to build up a thick coating. This is the same material mentioned in chapter 8, Lure Repair, in the section Rubber Coating.

Sharpening Stones

Sharpening stones for hooks and knives can become filled with metal filings, which makes them ineffective. Soak the stone in warm soapy water and scrub with a stiff brush to clean the filings from the stone and restore it to original, or close to original condition. To prevent more filings from collecting, apply a light oil to the sharpener whenever you use it to "float" the filings on the surface and prevent them from accumulating on the surface.

Landing Nets

Landing nets can usually be repaired when the net is torn or damaged and the handle or frame is broken or bent.

Bent frames can often be re-formed into their original shape. If the frame is cracked or broken, it must be spliced. Hacksaw through the frame at the break and insert a dowel into the frame here to repair it. You may have to round out the opening with a metal rod, pry bar, or similar tool to open an end crimped or closed by the break. If this is difficult, remove an inch or so of the frame from each side of the break or crack, then insert the dowel into the open ends. Use a straight-grain dowel for strength and, if possible, one that exactly fits the frame's aluminum tubing.

Make sure that the dowel fits about 1 to $1\frac{1}{2}$ inches into each side of the frame. To secure it in place, coat the dowel with epoxy and use a short, round-head screw (sheet-metal screws work fine) to fasten the cut frame to the dowel insert. For additional support, split a 3 to 4-inch-long section of aluminum tubing lengthwise, place it around the dowel/frame repair, and wrap with heavy cord as if it were a rod wrap, then coat with an epoxy finish.

Broken handles can be repaired the same way. The straight handles will allow 6-inch or longer dowel inserts on each side of the break, which will also provide more strength. Splicing the outside of aluminum tubing is also a good idea.

Nets can be repaired with heavy cord. The best material is waxed nylon cord

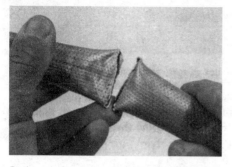

Broken shafts on aluminum landing nets can be repaired.

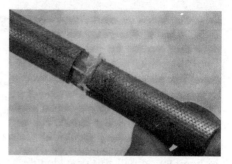

Use a dowel and glue it in place. Cord shims can be used, just as when replacing a reel seat or working on a bushing or shim for a ferrule (see chapter 6). Here a shimmed dowel is in place and glued.

Finished repair, with two screws holding the dowel in place.

made for net making, but lacking that, a heavy cord, rubbed with candle wax or soaked in melted wax, also works. The wax gives the cord some body so that knots will better be held in place. Waxed cord is also easier to tie in the special net knots needed.

To repair a hole in a net, first unfasten the frame at the handle/ hoop joint and remove the net. Stretch out the torn area of the net so that you can work on

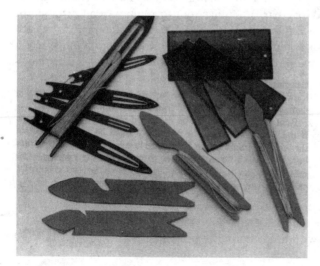

Examples of net shuttles, net gauges, and homemade cardboard shuttles. Different-sized shuttles are available for different-sized mesh, and naturally any size can be made from stiff cardboard or plastic. Because homemade shuttles are usually lightweight, the card should be wrapped on lightly to avoid bending the shuttle.

Net-repair knot used to
repair large sections of torn

it. Begin by tying the nylon cord to the last undamaged net loop at the upper left-hand area of the tear. Next, measure the size of the loop in the net, measuring straight down from the loop. It helps if you have a gauge to measure this distance, because you can use it to form new loops. Make a gauge from stiff cardboard and be sure it's the same width as the loop spacing.

Hold the cardboard horizontally in place at the lowest secure knot or undamaged loop, then bring the cord around the front of the spacer and up behind it. Now bring the cord up through the next loop, take it around behind the loop, then in front of the loop but through the space formed by the cord. (See illustrations.) In essence you are tying a sheet bend, a basic Boy Scout knot. Hold the cord tight and pull the knot secure.

Continue in this manner until the torn area in that row of loops is repaired. Then go down one row of loops and work right to left to continue the repair. Move back and forth, one row at a time, to repair the hole in the net. Tie off at the end with several half hitches.

Another way to repair a hole is to cut away the damaged area, measure it, and

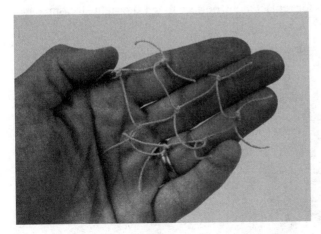

For large repairs, small
patches of net can be woven
and then knotted into place
in the hole, using a regular
overhand square knot.

then weave a net-repair "patch." The patch should be slightly smaller than the hole cut into the net so that one strand, or loop length, can run from the old net to the new patch to mend it. Then repeat as above, making the zigzag pattern and knots to fasten the new patch to the old net. The patch will be woven with cord and a loop gauge in the same technique as used for repairs. A simple shuttle made from light-weight plastic or heavy cardboard also helps make the knots and minimizes tangles.

Small net holes may be knotted together with short lengths of cord for a quick and easy repair.

Replacing Net Bags The first step to replacing a bag is to make sure the new net is the same size as the old one so that it will fit and hang properly. Then cut off the old net bag, and remove the net hoop from the handle. On aluminum nets, this is easily accomplished by unscrewing the hoop from the handle where it is attached. Take the new net bag and slip the doubled, top-mesh loops over the dismantled frame. If all the loops will not fit at once, slip them on one at a time and put on only to stretch the bag around the frame, before adding the rest of them.

Older wood frame or custom-made wood frame nets are made in one piece so the handle and hoop cannot be separated. There are, however, two net-bag replacement possibilities. Many net hoops have small holes drilled horizontally into the rim through which the upper mesh loops are fitted and secured with a cord that runs around the frame in a small groove. This type of net is easy to replace. Buy or make a net that has the same number of loops as that being replaced. This is important because the top loops and holes must match up.

Use a light-wire hook or doubled loop of monofilament to run the loops through each hole. If the holes in the net frame are large, use masking tape or a length of line to hold the loops in place. When all the loops are through the holes, run heavy cord or braided nylon through each loop around the net frame. Pull each loop tight against the cord and the frame edge. Tie the edge cord in a tight knot, preferably at the yoke of the frame, which will hide the knot.

If for some reason this won't work or the frame doesn't have any holes, wrap heavy cord around the frame and through each mesh loop to hold the bag in place.

When buying net bags for replacement, be sure to get the right size, since net

Old nets are held in place by the upper part of the net running through holes in the wood frame and held in place with a cord that runs around the perimeter of the net. These nets are also easily repaired.

bags will vary from small for short-handled trout nets, to large bags for long-handled large-fish boat nets.

Gaffs

Most gaffs have hooks securely fastened to aluminum shafts and should not need to be repaired. Some gaffs still have wood handles, though; these can be replaced if broken. To replace a handle, cut through the wire wraps or metal sleeve that holds the hook to the handle. Remove the gaff hook. A gaff hook has a long shank, like a fish hook, with a right-angle bend at its end to hold it in the handle and prevent it from pulling loose.

You can attach this hook to a new gaff handle, if available, or any strong handle. The best handles are made of hickory for garden tools. Whether you need a lightweight hoe handle or a heavy, thick shovel handle will depend upon the size of the fish and the size of the gaff hook.

To prepare the handle for the gaff, cut off any sharp taper or slotted end designed for tools. Then fasten the handle into a workshop vise and, using a chisel, whittle a groove in the end that is deep, long, and wide enough to just hold the gaff shank. Do not make it too loose. At the upper end of the slot, drill a short hole to hold the right-angle bend of the shank end. Fit the gaff hook into the slot. To hold the hook in place, use utility wire (available at hardware stores) to wrap the length of the shank, just as you would wrap a guide on a rod. Begin by wrapping the wire over itself at the lower end. Wrap to the upper end. Beyond the end of the hook, put a small round-head screw into the handle but do not screw it all the way into the handle; wrap up to the screw. Cut the wire, wrap it around the handle, and tighten the screw to fasten the wire.

For a quick down-and-dirty method of doing the same thing, use two or three hose fasteners. These are also sold in hardware stores.

Stringers

The cord on most stringers wears out eventually. Get a 6-foot length of $\frac{1}{8}$-inch cable (look in the chain section of any hardware store) and two crimping sleeves or fasteners. Remove the hooks from the old cord and slide them on the new cable. Put a large welded ring at each end of the cable and secure them in place with the fasteners or crimping sleeves.

Rod Cases

Aluminum rod cases are almost indestructible. They can suffer from dents and dings from travel, however. Usually these are no more than cosmetic damages, but occasionally, a deep dent might interfere with a rod guide. To remove or reduce dents, get a 5- to 6-foot section of closet rod the same size or slightly smaller than the tube diameter. (Wood closet rods usually come in $1\frac{1}{16}$-, $1\frac{1}{4}$-, and $1\frac{3}{8}$-inch diameters.) Slip the wood rod in the case, then gently hammer the dented area as the closet rod acts as a backstop. Keep the rod case vertical and supported on the floor when doing this. By doing this, you are using the closet rod as an internal hammer to push out the dent.

This won't completely take the dent out, however, unless the closet rod and inside diameter of the rod case match. To remove more of the dent, tightly wrap the closet rod with cord until it is almost snug in the case. Then tap on the rod case a little at a time to remove more of the dent.

Even after doing this, you will still have a remnant of the dent, but the rod case will be functional.

You can also remove dents by putting the closet rod or an iron pipe horizontally into a vise, then run the rod tube onto the pipe or rod, and use a rubber or plastic mallet to gently hammer the dent out. The pipe or rod works as an anvil to take out the dent. For larger dents, work around the perimeter of the dent first then on the center. To do this, you *must* have the pipe or rod clamped securely into a vise that *must* be firmly mounted on a workbench to prevent the pipe or rod from moving as you hammer.

Waders and Boots

There are several wader materials and each requires a different type of repair. Rubber, rubber-coated canvas, and rubberized nylon are all repaired with a kit containing patch material and a rubber-type cement.

Because of the thinness of the material used in waders, a patch is almost always necessary. Before making any repairs, thoroughly dry the wader or boot inside and out. This is critical to bonding the cement and patch. For small punctures, such as might be made on barbed wire, first cut a patch to cover the damaged area. A patch should usually be at least $\frac{1}{2}$ to 1-inch larger on all sides than the punctured area. (A small puncture, therefore, would need a 1- to 2-inch-square patch.)

Most wader and hip boot manufacturers include a small repair kit with their products. Follow their instructions in repairing boots. These instructions generally include the following:

1. To prepare the surface for patching, use the small abrader, which comes with the patch kit, to thoroughly roughen or sand the surface. Lacking the abrader, use sandpaper, file, or rasp. Make sure that this area is at least the size and shape of the patch.
2. Once clean, spread a rubber or rubber-based cement on the abraded area. Spread and allow to dry.
3. When dry, peel the protective covering from the patch and place the patch over the hole. Make sure it is positioned properly, because once it's in contact with the cement, you will not be able to move it.

For larger holes, use a bigger patch. To ensure the mend, repair the inside of the boot in the same manner, so you have a sandwich of patching.

If your kit does not have properly sized individual patches, you can use the larger sheeting material, supplied by most manufacturers. Cut the patch and round

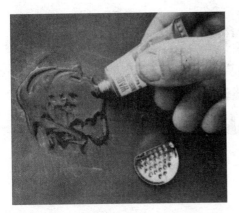

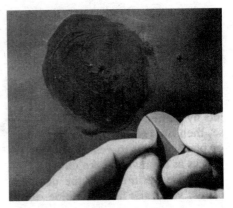

Repairing waders or hippers by abrading the surface of the leak and then adding rubber cement. Most waders come with a repair kit for this.

Allow the glue to dry and then peel back the self-adhesive patch.

Putting the patch in place.

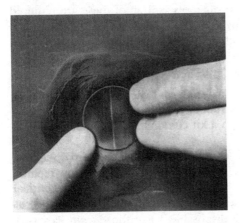

the edges. Do not remove the protective coating when doing this. Some manufacturers have patches of various materials. For example, Hodgman supplies a repair kit that includes rubber, canvas OD, and canvas camouflage patches with their rubber, nylon, and canvas waders.

Neoprene material used in most waders is 3mm or $\frac{1}{8}$ inch thick, so cement is adequate for all repairs. A neoprene-based cement is supplied in their repair kits. To repair small pinholes, first find the hole and completely dry the material. Then, from the inside, press outward on the pinhole to expose and enlarge it to make it visible. Put cement in the hole and relax the fabric. When cured, the cement will bond with the neoprene to make a watertight seal. Larger holes can be repaired the same way.

The Fisherman's Tool Kit

THE TOOLS THAT YOU NEED to maintain and repair tackle are minimal. What you use will vary with the tackle being repaired. Most of these tools you will have or can obtain easily at low cost. If you get into tackle repair extensively, you will need more and better tools to cope with the range of tackle.

The following is a complete list of repair tools. Not all of these are required for simple or onetime repairs. When repairing a rod, for example, you will need only razor blades, brushes, a rasp, file, sandpaper, and a burnisher. With those tools you can rewrap any rod guide and repair any handle, grip, or reel seat. For most reel repairs, you will need only a set of small screwdrivers, a small wrench, and the repair tool that came with the reel.

Rod Repair Tools

Rod repair tools are similar to those used for rod building. What you need depends upon the extent of repairs you wish to do. The tools needed are simple and include:

Brushes For adding epoxy and color preserver when recoating or finishing rod wraps. Best brushes are inexpensive and disposable. I like those from Flex Coat because the bristles are bound into the tip end so that they cannot come out and mar a finish.

Razor Blades Razor blades are a must for removing old wraps and finish from a blank and trimming excess thread when completing a new wrap. Best and cheapest are the boxes of industrial single-edge blades.

Heat Source A heat source, or sources, is needed for several tasks including removing a tiptop, metal butt caps, reel seats, and metal ferrules. When removing a tiptop, it's hard to beat a disposable butane lighter. For larger tasks, a laboratory-type alcohol lamp has a clean flame and works well. A propane torch may be needed for tasks such as removing metal ferrules on offshore rods and metal reel seats.

Emery Board Ideal for removing the last vestiges of old epoxy on guide wraps.

Round File Useful for roughing up the inside of reel seats and butt caps for better glue adhesion, and for enlarging the hole in cork rings when replacing grips.

Tiptop Gauge This isn't necessary to repair a rod, but it is a handy tool to have for repairing and building rods. The tiptop gauge is a flat plastic rule with molded pegs to fit tiptops from $\frac{4}{64}$ to $\frac{32}{64}$ inch in size. The gauge makes it possible to easily check tiptops when you want to buy another in the same size. A gauge also measures the tip diameter of a rod when the last few inches break off. Gauges are available through most of the do-it-yourself tackle catalogs.

Internal calipers can also measure a removed tiptop; external calipers can measure the tip of the rod blank.

Guide Gauges As with tiptop gauges, these are not necessary but are helpful. Simple gauges are just a chart that shows the diameter of guide rings in millimeters and inches. A second type of gauge measures the ring diameter of a removed guide.

Rasps These are rougher than files and come in many shapes. Flat rasps are best. Rasps are ideal for rough-shaping cork grips, before filing and sanding.

Files Coarse or bastard-cut files are also good for shaping cork grips. Best are 8 to 10 inches long.

Sandpaper Sandpaper, garnet paper, or emery cloth is necessary when doing the final shaping and smoothing of cork grips. Coarse, medium-fine, and extra-fine grades are needed.

Rod Wrapper These tools are sold by some tackle shops and mail-order houses. Usually made of wood, they consist of a base, two supports to hold the rod, and a thread-tension device. They are definitely not necessary for occasional repairs, although they do make them easier. You can make a wrapper using scrap pine shelving for a base, two 6- to 8-inch lengths tacked to the base's end with a V-cut in the top of the board as supports, and a sewing machine thread-tension device to control the thread spool.

Another tension device uses a $\frac{1}{4}$-20 bolt in the base, which holds the thread at the proper tension with a compression spring and wing nut. Plastic washers, cut from a plastic milk bottle, prevent thread from binding. Still another alternative is to use two $\frac{1}{4}$-20 eye bolts through the base, 3 inches on center, with a $\frac{1}{4}$-inch rod through the eye bolts to hold the thread. Use a spring, washer, and wing nut underneath to adjust the tension. For these rigs, you must have additional feet under the base so that the bolts clear the working table.

Grip Seater One of the problems with seating new synthetic grips is that they must be forced onto the blank because the hole in the grip is, by necessity, smaller than the blank. A grip seater facilitates this procedure. The seater is simply a piece of 4-inch-wide shelving with a hole drilled into its center. The hole should be slightly larger than the diameter of the blank. Use the seater to push the grip easily into place on the blank. You can also make a more elaborate grip seater, with different holes in the board that fit several sizes of grip/blank combinations.

Cork Clamp These clamps are used to hold cork while glue is drying, such as when replacing rings on a cork grip. Clamps can be improvised. Roger Seiders of Flex Coat suggests using a cored brick (these are for wall construction, not paving) or a 5-pound weight from a barbell set. The brick or weight is placed over the blank after the cork grip is glued, then the rod is placed vertically so that the weight presses the cork rings together. Handle the brick carefully so you won't inadvertently scratch the rod.

Cork clamps made just for gluing rod grips are available, but you can also make your own. To make one, you need two pieces of 2- or 3-inch-wide by 6- to 8-inch-long shelving, two lengths of ¼-20 All-Thread (length determined by the length of the grips made or repaired), two ¼-20 wing nuts, six washers, and four ¼-20 nuts. Drill a ¾-inch hole through the center of one board, then drill a ⅜-inch hole 1 inch from each end. Drill ¼-inch holes 1 inch from each end of the second board (so they will align with the small holes on the first board). Use four nuts and four of the washers to fasten the two lengths of All-Thread to this board. The other board is slipped over the All-Thread, followed by the washers and wing nuts. In use, a rod blank with a freshly glued grip is placed in the clamp, the rod extending through the hole in the free end. Any length can be made, based on the rod handle length.

An alternative is to use a pipe clamp to exert pressure on the grip. To do this, use a C-clamp to fasten a short length of wood shelving to each jaw of the pipe clamp. Drill a hole in the exposed end of one board. Place the rod between these temporary wood jaws, with the rod blank extending through the hole in the one board. Tighten the pipe clamp slightly to exert pressure. Do not overtighten, because these clamps could easily apply too much pressure.

Burnisher Burnishers smooth thread wraps after rewrapping a guide. Special burnishers are available, and the one for transferring letters in drafting, manufactured by the C-Thru Ruler Company, is ideal. Smooth plastic pens or similar items make fine substitutes.

Rod-Curing Motor Available from tackle shops and mail-order houses, these are slow-turning motors with a device to hold the butt end of the rod. They constantly rotate the rod so that epoxy won't sag and run. Most motors have 1- to 60-rpm speed.

Excellent home-built machines can easily be made. Attach a 2-inch PVC pipe cap to the motor shaft to hold the rod. To do this, first drill and tap three ¼-20 holes at three equal points around the edge or lip of the cap. Fit these with 2-inch-long thumbscrews or eye bolts to hold the rod. Fasten the cup (glue or use bolts on a threaded motor shaft) to the motor and mount the motor on a small stand. Use another stand with a V-cut to support the other end of the rod. Line the V with plastic from disposable bottles or cartons to protect the rod. A simpler rod support is made from a small cardboard box with a V-cut at the top.

A quick down-and-dirty rod-curing device can be made from a slow-rpm rotisserie motor. These motors have square holes for fitting the barbecue spit. A square wood plug force-fitted into the hole makes it possible to screw the PVC cup to the motor.

Drill and Drill Bits These are rarely needed for rod repairs, but are necessary to drill through loose reels seats to insert pins. A small variable-power drill with $\frac{1}{32}$- to $\frac{1}{8}$-inch bits works well. Exact size is determined by the pin and reel seat.

Reel Repair Tools

As with rod repairs, the tools needed for reel repair are simple. In most cases, all you need to clean, maintain, and lightly repair a reel are the tools that came with it. Because these are simple and cheap combinations, higher-quality tools are best for extensive reel work.

Reel Mate This Bass Pro Shops bracket is a support stand that clamps a reel in place when repairing or lubing. It also holds a spool of line, which facilitates changing line.

Line Winders Line winders by Berkley, Reel Boy, and Lineminder are available to spool line on spinning, spincast, and casting reels. The Berkley mounts on a table, counter, or workbench; the Lineminder clamps to the rod to transfer line from any size of spool. A new consumer portable electric line winder, to spool line on spinning, baitcast, and fly reels, is being developed by Triangle Manufacturing Co. at this writing.

Reel Tool Most of these are small, flat, and a combination screwdriver and wrench. They are designed to work on the screws and fasteners on a specific reel. They are awkward to hold for extended use, so more precise tools are better. These are ideal for tacklebox and field use.

Screwdrivers You need small sizes for reels in both regular and Phillips heads. Get a set of these in the small sizes that fit reels. Moody, RadioShack, and many other companies make screwdrivers specifically for small, precise work. I use a RadioShack set of 16 tools, which includes regular and Phillips screwdrivers and small hex socket wrenches.

Screwdrivers are a must to remove side plates, tighten loose spinning bails, remove and replace pawls from casting reels, adjust clicks on fly reels, and so on.

Wrenches Wrenches are often included in screwdriver sets, but small open-end box wrenches are also available, along with tiny adjustable wrenches. Some of these are really working toys, but they are ideal for dismantling reels.

Awls An awl is nothing more than a point, which is handy for depositing oil in small recesses, helping to hook tension springs over holding hooks or pins, and so on. A small awl can be made from a thick darning needle fitted onto a wood dowel handle.

Oilers Oilers and greasers are small specialty tools that usually come with the oil or grease. Most are almost penlike—with a removable cap and a hollow needle applicator. Their small size makes them ideal for lubricating reels and other fishing tackle.

Ring Pliers These are small pliers with straight or angled pinpoints, used to remove and attach internal or external ring fasteners. Regular pliers, carefully used, serve the same purpose. In addition, many of the small ring fasteners used in fishing reels don't have the small end holes that allow use of these specialized pliers. So don't buy ring pliers until you need them. Good ring pliers are available from hardware and automotive-supply stores.

Lure Repair Tools

Lure tools are needed for repainting, replacing hooks, polishing, and so on.

Hook Sharpeners Hook sharpeners are maintenance rather than repair tools. Hook sharpening is so important, however, that hook sharpeners are included.
There are many styles and types of hook sharpeners available. They include:

1. Files: Large 8- to 10-inch-long files are best to quickly sharpen large hooks, because they will remove the maximum amount of metal in the shortest amount of time. Double-cut files cut better than single cut.
2. Diamond hones: Hones are available from Diamond Machining Technology, Eze-Lap, Gaines, Bass Pro Shops, and other companies. Diamond Machining Technology offers several diamond hook hones, including a long-handled hone, a small hone shaped to look like a key, and flat hones for hooks and knives. Eze-Lap has small hones in fine, medium, and coarse grits. Gaines and Bass Pro Shops sell a small pen-sized diamond hone with a penlike cap.
3. Rotary grinders: Examples of these vary greatly. There is the Point Maker by Texas Tackle, which is a bench or boat-operated, thin grinding wheel: AC for home use and DC (cigarette lighter adapter) models for boat or RV use are available. Johnson and Berkley both make battery-operated (AA or C) rotary stones.

Brushes Brushes are a must for most painting or touch-up jobs. The fast-drying field-use paints usually have brushes in the bottle lid. Testor's has felt-tip applicators. Other paints will require a brush. Disposable brushes are ideal.

Pliers Pliers are good for holding lures for painting, removing and replacing hooks, adjusting diving lips, and so on. Handy pliers include the compound-action pliers on the Sargent design, and long-nose pliers (especially for painting).

Scale Netting Scale netting is ideal for reproducing or replacing scale finishes on lures. Fine- and coarse-scale netting is available from tackle shops and mail-order companies. Lacking that, you can always buy tulle or similar netting in craft and fabric shops.

Netting Frame Netting must be held slightly against the lure when spraying a scale finish. One easy, no-mess way to do this is to hold the netting in a frame. A wood frame can be made for this, stapling the netting to it, although the spring-clamp embroidery frames, available in craft or needlepoint shops, are ideal.

Heat Source A heat source is needed to melt soft-plastic lures to either rejoin them or to make new lures. Disposable cigarette lighters or small alcohol lamps serve this purpose well.

Wire Cutters Wire cutters are handy for trimming plastic, metal, blades, lips, wires, and skirts on lures. Cutters can also be used to cut bent wires on spinner-baits and buzzbaits before repairing or converting them to short-arm lures. They can also be used to trim blades and lips on lures.

Split-Ring Pliers Split-ring pliers are necessary to anyone who is seriously inter-ested in lure repair. These long-nose pliers have a small tooth at the end of one jaw, which springs open the split ring. The pliers are the only safe way to remove and replace hooks on split rings.

Knives are often suggested for opening rings, but this is dangerous because you can easily cut yourself. Split-ring pliers are available in inexpensive stamped-out styles and more sturdily constructed models.

Tools for Tackleboxes, Accessories

Tools for repairing tackleboxes and accessories are minimal. What is broken often dictates the tool you use to fix it.

Drill and Drill Bits The same tool you need to repair reel seats can also be used to drill out rivets holding hinges, latches, and so on before replacing with new parts.

Pop Rivet Tool These are ideal for tackle repair, including replacement of parts on tackleboxes, reriveting net frames on handles, fixing bait buckets, and so on.

Hollow Needle A large hypodermic needle is ideal for making nail knots to con-nect leader butts and fly lines. Use a size 15 and file the end so it's blunt to pre-vent accidents.

Clippers Nail clippers are ideal for cutting line and trimming soft-plastic worms, plastic toothbrush-type weedguards, and other lures. Keep these and the hollow needle on a lanyard so they are readily accessible.

Net Gauges Not necessary but handy if you tear up nets; these usually come in sets but can be bought individually. They are nothing more than rectangular plastic sheets that ensure net loops are consistently sized. Eight sizes are available. You can make a gauge from scrap material, such as thick cardboard. The gauge should be 6 to 8 inches long; the width will be determined by the size of the net loop to repair.

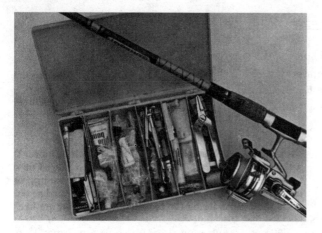

A special field repair kit.

Net Shuttles Net shuttles are pointed and have brackets to wrap and hold net cord used to make net loops. They come in nine sizes. You can make them using stiff cardboard, as shown on page 96. Both net gauges and shuttles are available from Jann's NetCraft, Inc.

Field Repair Kits

It would be nice to think that, barring accidents, and providing tackle is kept in good repair, field repairs are unnecessary. That's not realistic, however, because tackle does break. For longer trips, take a field kit. My practice is to carry an oiler, reel tool, and other minimal repair tools and extra tackle on local trips. On trips that might take me away from tackle supplies briefly (such as a weekend backpacking trip), I carry a repair and tool kit that fits into a $6 \times 4 \times 1$-inch plastic lure box. On longer trips—to Alaska, abroad, or into the backwoods for a week or so—I take a more comprehensive kit that fits into a $10 \times 6 \times 1\frac{3}{4}$-inch box.

Suggested contents for this kit include tools and materials for simple repairs that can be easily accomplished in the field. The amount and number of items you pack depend upon the size of the kit. The following is based on the larger kit that I carry (the smaller kit is a scaled-down version) based on immediate needs and the tackle used.

Each compartment (there are usually six in these small boxes) is filled with specific parts, as follows:

Compartment 1: This compartment holds grease, oil, and wax. The items are kept in a small plastic sandwich bag to protect the rest of the repair kit should any of the items leak. Carry oils and grease for lubing reels, and a small piece of candle wax for assuring good fit on the ferrule. Fly-line cleaners can also be packed here.

Compartment 2: Glues are kept in this second section. They should include instant (Crazy) glues, Pliobond (for sealing nail knots), and five-minute epoxy.

Compartment 3: Many reels come with a small container filled with parts most

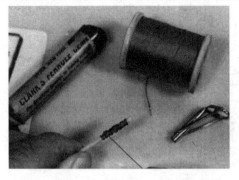

Spare tiptops should be carried in any field repair kit, but not all sizes are needed. For a temporary repair, a tiptop can be built up with thread as shown to match the size of a replacement tiptop.

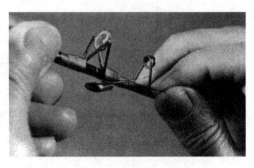

For a quick repair when everything else is lacking, a safety pin can be bent and used as a replacement guide.

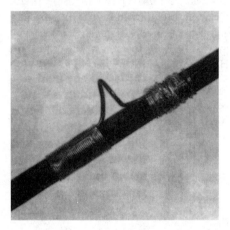

In the field, guide wraps can be done with monofilament line. Left, neat for a semipermanent job, right, quick for a one-day patch job.

often needed and most easily replaced on spinning, casting, and saltwater reels. These include springs, brake blocks, pawls, bail springs, screws, drag washers, and so on. Include these parts for all the reels that you have or are likely to take on that trip.

Compartment 4: Rod parts. Include replacement tiptops (such as oversize sets designed to fit almost any rod); Aetna types that are wrapped in place; and guides of several sizes and styles to fit the different rods that you carry.

Compartment 5: Repair materials. This section should include rod-wrapping thread, tape, sandpaper, and so on.

Compartment 6: Tools. This section should include the tools that came with your reels, a set of regular and Phillips-head screwdrivers, one or two small wrenches, awl, split-ring pliers, small knife, ignition file, and any other tools you need for your rod, reel, and tackle repair.

Tackle Manufacturers

U NFORTUNATELY, too few of us keep the vital owner's manual, service list-
ing, parts list, and warranty information that come with all new reels and
much other new tackle. If you are going to do your own reel repairs, or
wish to check the warranty information on a rod, you *must* have the appropriate
information. When servicing reels, schematic assembly drawings and parts lists are
a must for ordering the right parts. If this information is lost, copies are usually
available from the manufacturer. In all requests, be sure to include all important
data, including part number, model, and serial numbers on the rod or reel.

Abel Reels
165 Aviador Street
Camarillo, CA 93010
(805) 484-8789

Abu Garcia
Outdoor Technologies
   Group
1900 18th Street
Spirit Lake, IA 51360
(712) 336-1520

AFTCO Manufacturing Co.,
   Inc.
17351 B Murphy Avenue
Irvine, CA 92614
(714) 660-8757

All Star Graphite Rods, Inc.
9817 Whithorn
Houston, TX 77095
(713) 855-9603

Bass Pro Shops
2500 East Kearney
Springfield, MO 65898
(800) 227-7776

Berkley
Outdoor Technologies
   Group
1900 18th Street
Spirit Lake, IA 51360
(712) 336-1520

Biscayne Rod Manufacturing
   Co.
425 East Ninth Street
Hialeah, FL 33010
(305) 884-0808

Browning Fishing
Brunswick Outdoor Recre-
   ation Group
6101 East Apache
Box 840
Tulsa, OK 74101-0840
(918) 836-0316

Cabela's
812 13th Avenue
Sidney, NE 69160
(308) 234-5555

Cortland Line Co.
3736 Kellogg Road
Box 5588
Cortland, NY 13045
(607) 756-2851

Daiwa Corporation
12851 Midway Place
Cerritos, CA 90703
(562) 802-9589

Dolphin Electreel, Inc.
2819 62nd Avenue East
Bradenton, FL 34203
(941) 751-2919

Eagle Electronics
Box 669
Catoosa, OK 74015
(918) 437-6881

Electric Fishing Reel Systems, Inc.
1700 Sullivan Street
Box 20411 (Zip 27420)
Greensboro, NC 27405
(910) 273-9101

Falcon Graphite Rods
821 West Elgin
Broken Arrow, OK 74012
(918) 251-0020

Fenwick
Outdoor Technologies
  Group
1900 18th Street
Spirit Lake, IA 51360
(712) 336-1520

Fin-Nor
United Sports Specialists
  Corporation
5553 Anglers Avenue
Suite 109-110
Fort Lauderdale, FL 33312
(954) 966-5507

Fish Hawk Electronics Corporation
Box 340
Crystal Lake, IA 60039
(815) 363-0929

Furuno U.S.A., Inc.
271 Harbor Way
Box 2343
South San Francisco, CA
  94083
(415) 873-9393

G. Loomis, Inc.
1359 Downriver Drive
Woodland, WA 98674
(360) 225-6516

HT Enterprises, Inc.
139 East Sheboygan Street
Box 909
Campbellsport, WI 53010
(414) 533-5080

Johnson, Johnson Worldwide
  Associates
Fishing and Marine
1326 Willow Road
Sturtevant, WI 53177
(414) 884-1500

L.L. Bean
Casco Street
Freeport, ME 04033
(800) 809-7057

Lamiglas, Inc.
1400 Atlantic
Box U
Woodland, WA 98674
(360) 225-9436

Lew's
Brunswick Outdoor Recreation Group
6101 East Apache
Box 840
Tulsa, OK 74101-0840
(918) 836-0316

Lowrance Electronics
12,000 East Skelly Drive
Tulsa, OK 74128
(918) 437-6881

Magellan Systems Corporation
960 Overland Court
San Dimas, CA 91773
(909) 394-5000

Marado, Inc.
19247 80th Avenue South
Kent, WA 98032
(253) 395-3355

Martin
Brunswick Outdoor Recreation Group
6101 East Apache
Box 270
Tulsa OK 74101
(918) 836-5581

Mitchell
Johnson Worldwide Associates
Fishing and Marine
1326 Willow Road
Sturtevant, WI 53177
(414) 884-1500

Ocean Tech Company, Inc.,
  U.S.A.
2822 Metropolitan Place
Pomona, CA 91767
(909) 596-9858

Okuma Fishing Tackle
580 Lambert Road
Suite F
Brea, CA 92821
(714) 990-3779

Orvis Company
Route 7A
Manchester, VT 05254
(800) 333-1550

Penn Fishing Tackle Manufacturing Co.
3028 West Hunting Park
  Avenue
Philadelphia, PA 19132-1121
(215) 229-9415

Pinnacle
Silver Star Co., Ltd.
1141 Silstar Road
Box 6505
West Columbia, SC 29171
(803) 794-8521

Pinpoint Positioning Systems
Pinpoint Corp.
1124 South Lewis Avenue
Tulsa, OK 74104
(918) 584-6500

Quantum
Brunswick Outdoor Recre-
    ation Group
6101 East Apache
Box 270
Tulsa OK 74101
(918) 836-5581

Red Wolf
Outdoor Technologies
    Group
1900 18th Street
Spirit Lake, IA 51360
(712) 336-1520

Sage
8500 NE Day Road
Bainbridge Island, WA 98110
(206) 842-6608

Scientific Anglers
3M Corp.
223-4NE-05
3M Center
St. Paul, MN 55144-1000
(612) 733-4751

Shakespeare Co.
3801 Westmore Drive
Columbia, SC 29223
(803) 754-7000

Shimano American Corp.
1 Holland Drive
Irvine, CA 92618
(714) 951-5003

Silstar Corporation of
    America
Silver Star Co., Ltd.
1141 Silstar Road
Box 6505
West Columbia, SC 29171
(803) 794-8521

South Bend Sporting Goods
1950 Stanley Street
Northbrook, IL 60065
(847) 715-1400

St. Croix Rods
856 4th Avenue North
Box 279
Park Falls, WI 54552
(715) 762-3226

Star Rods
8538 NW 64th Street
Miami, FL 33166
(305) 592-3134

Aurora
Superior Sports Products
    (USA) Inc.
Box 958725
Hoffman Estates, IL 60195-
    8725

Swede Industries, Inc.
2800 South Peterson Road
Claremore, OK 74017
(918) 342-1977

Wright & McGill Co.
4245 East 46th Avenue
Box 16011
Denver, CO 80216
(303) 321-1481

Zebco
Brunswick Outdoor Recre-
    ation Group
6101 East Apache
Box 270
Tulsa OK 74101
(918) 836-5581

Catalog Suppliers

Angler's Workshop
1350 Atlantic
Woodland, WA 98674

Angling Specialties
19520 McLoughlin Boulevard
Gladstone, OR 97027

Barlow's Tackle Shop
451 North Central Expressway
Box 369
Richardson, TX 75080

Bass Pro Shops
2500 East Kearny
Springfield, MO 65898
(800-227-7776)

Bunda's Quality Tackle Components
Box 162
Nashotah, WI 53058

Cabela's
812 13th Avenue
Sidney, NE 69160

Custom Tackle Supply
2559 Highway 41-A South
Shelbyville, TN 37160

Dakota Tackle
2001 Bismarck Expressway
Bismarck, ND 58504

Dale Clemens
444 Schantz Road
Allentown, PA 18104

Do-It Molds
501 North State Street
Denver, IA 50622

E. Hille
The Angler's Supply House
Box 896
Williamsport, PA 17703

El Capitan
1590 NW 27th Avenue
Miami, FL 33125

Feather-Craft
Box 19904
St. Louis, MO 63144

Great Rip Tackle
Box 3646
Cranston, RI 02910

Hilts Molds
1461 East Lake Mead Drive
Henderson, NY 89015

Industrial Art Supply
5724 West 36th Street
Minneapolis, MN 55416

NetCraft
Jann's Sportsman's Supplies
Box 4315
Toledo, OH 43609

Jerry's Tackle Shop
604 12th Street
Highland, IL 62249-1820

JoCo
2301 Galilee
Zion, IL 60099

Kaufmann's Streamborn
Box 23032
Portland, OR 97223

Mac's Shark River Tackle
1301 Highway 35
Neptune, NJ 07753

Madison River Fishing Company
Box 627
109 Main Street
Ennis, MT 59729

Midland Tackle Company
66 Route 17
Sloatsburg, NY 10974

Shoff Tackle Supply
Box 1227
Kent, WA 98035-1227

Sportsmans Guide
965 Decatur Avenue North
Golden Valley, MN 55427

The Surfcaster
113 Maywood Road
Box 1731
Darien, CT 06820-1731

Tackle Craft
1440 Kennedy Road
Box 280
Chippewa Falls, WI 54729

Tackle Service Center
246 East Washington
Mooresville, IN 46158

West Falmouth Tackle
Box 873
West Falmouth, MA 02574

Index